The Express Guides

The Express and Kogan Page have joined forces to publish a series of practical guides offering no-nonsense advice on a wide range of financial, legal and business topics.

Whether you want to manage your money better, make more money, get a new business idea off the ground – and make sure it's legal – there's an Express Guide for you.

Titles published so far are:

Great Ideas for Making Money
Niki Chesworth

Your Money
How to Make the Most of it
(Second Edition)
Niki Chesworth

Buying a Property Abroad
A Practical Guide for Overseas Homebuyers
(Second Edition)
Niki Chesworth

You and the Law
A Simple Guide to All Your Legal Problems
Susan Singleton

How to Cut Your Tax Bill Without Breaking the Law
(Third Edition)
Grant Thornton, Chartered Accountants

Be Your Own Boss
How to Set Up a Successful Small Business
David McMullan

Readymade Business Letters That Get Results
(Second Edition)
Jim Douglas

The Woman's Guide to Finance
How to Manage all your Money Matters
(Second Edition)
Tony Levene

Buying Your First Franchise
(Second Edition)
G R Clarke

The Express Investment Guide
Practical Advice for Making the Right Choice
(Second Edition)
Tony Levene

Network Marketing
An Introductory Guide
David Barber

How to Sell More
A Guide for Small Business
Neil Johnson

Your Home Office
A Practical Guide to Using Technology Successfully
(Revised Second Edition)
Peter Chatterton

How to Cope with Separation and Divorce
David Green

Available from all good bookshops, or to obtain further information please contact the publishers at the address below:

Kogan Page Ltd
120 Pentonville Rd
LONDON N1 9JN
Tel: 0171-278 0433
Fax: 0171-837 6348

Acknowledgements

I would like to thank all those who have helped me to produce this book, particularly my co-author Sascha Olofson for her excellent research skills and for translating tax and legal documents from Spanish, Italian and French.

In addition I found the following organisations and individuals most helpful and hope you will too:

FOPDAC — the Federation of Overseas Property Developers, Agents and Consultants.

Steve Emmett of international estate agents Brian A French & Associates for his helpful information on Italy and Greece.

John Hart from A House in France Ltd and Christine Hilton from La Residence for information on the French property market.

Dr Claudio Del Giudice for his Italian tax expertise.

David Scott of David Scott International for his advice on property in Spain and John Howell for his legal expertise.

Cornish & Co solicitors for very useful guides to Malta, Cyprus, Portugal and Gibraltar.

Bill Hartman of Hartman Homes in Florida, Arlette Adler from Villas Abroad for her extensive knowledge on Switzerland and Andorra, Michael Clare of Clare Developments for information on Greece and also accountants Blackstone Franks, which specialises in overseas taxation and property buying.

THE EXPRESS
BUYING A PROPERTY ABROAD

A Practical Guide for Overseas Homebuyers

SECOND EDITION

NIKI CHESWORTH
AND
SASCHA OLOFSON

Warning: Information contained in this book is subject to change but is as accurate as can be at time of publication. As so many countries are covered and taxation changes every year it is impossible to be up to date on every aspect of tax. However, where governments have announced plans to change laws and tax rates in the future these have been included. Exchange rates used in calculating property prices are those at time of going to press and are subject to fluctuation.

Kogan Page Limited, The Express and the author cannot assume legal responsibility for the accuracy of any particular statement in this work. No responsibility for loss or damage occasioned to any person acting or refraining from action as a result of the material in this publication can be accepted by the authors or publishers.

First published in 1995
Second edition 1997

Apart from any fair dealing for the purposes of research or private study, or criticism or review, as permitted under the Copyright, Designs and Patents Act, 1988, this publication may only be reproduced, stored or transmitted, in any form or by any means, with the prior permission in writing of the publishers, or in the case of reprographic reproduction in accordance with the terms of licences issued by the Copyright Licensing Agency. Enquiries concerning reproduction outside those terms should be sent to the publishers at the undermentioned address:

Kogan Page Limited
120 Pentonville Road
London N1 9JN
© Niki Chesworth and Express Newspapers plc, 1995, 1997

British Library Cataloguing in Publication Data
A CIP record for this book is available from the British Library.

ISBN 0 7494 2017 0

Typeset by Saxon Graphics Ltd, Derby
Printed in England by Clays Ltd, St Ives plc

Contents

Acknowledgements		2
Introduction		9
Part I	**General Guidelines on Buying a Property Abroad**	**11**
1	Is buying a property overseas the right thing for me?	13
2	Can I really afford to buy a property abroad?	16
3	Alternative ways to buy a home overseas	19
4	What you need to know about buying a second/holiday home	22
5	Retiring abroad	26
6	Taking your children with you	29
7	Practical problems in moving	32
8	Who you need to tell	34
9	Making the most of your money – tax, benefits and avoiding expensive pitfalls	36
Part II	**A Country-by-Country Guide to Buying Your Property Abroad**	**41**
	Spain	43
	France	77
	Italy	109
	Portugal	123
	Greece	134
	The USA – Florida	140
	Other countries of interest to British homebuyers	148
	Useful addresses	160
Index		179
Index of Advertisers		187

"I'm sorry, Sir, your flight has just left!"

"What?" I looked at the girl at the checking desk in bewilderment – I was early! My flight did not leave until 6.45 pm and the time was only 5pm!

"I'm afraid that your flight was scheduled for 1645 and the plane has just taken off."

The girl looked very sorry and I looked very foolish. I just had to get to London that night as I had a very important appointment early the following morning. I needn't have worried. All I had to do was ask what I should do next and believe me, within 20 minutes and 10 helpful people later, I was safely booked on another flight leaving at 7pm. I said 10 helpful people later because I got on the next flight with the help of lots of good suggestions and charitable actions from the very personal and English speaking airport staff.

But this was not so unusual. One of the most striking things I noticed throughout my stay in Malta was that I found friendly and helpful people wherever I went. Although I was a foreigner in a foreign country, at no point did I feel in any way lost or helpless – an extremely positive point to note abut the Maltese islands.

So, what else can one say about Malta other than the friendly people? Well, the food is good and varied and not too expensive. English is the second language so it was very easy to communicate. The weather was absolutely fabulous, as were the crystal clear surrounding seas. Health facilities are excellent and free! and property was very good value and varied.

As I intended settling permanently abroad and had heard that taxation for foreign residents in Malta, was very reasonable, I asked a well established estate agency for some details on residency. Taxation, in fact, proved to be as little as 15% tax on income brought into the island if I became a permanent resident. To qualify as a resident I only had to bring in Stg12,600 per annum! Malta as a tax haven was excellent for me and my family.

I was also taken round to view a selection of properties in various price ranges to see if any suited my requirements – no problem there. The properties I was shown round were varied, so were the prices; from old houses of character, to modern apartments with sea views, to luxury villas. In fact, I shall be back later next month to review a selection of houses of character. I look forward to this very much but next time round I don't intend missing my flight!

Frank Salt (Real Estate) Ltd were my agents in Malta and Gozo and they took me round all the properties I wishes to see under no obligation at all. The company offers many services and also take care of all legal and administrative matters relating to the purchase of properties.

Retiring in Malta

Excellent conditions for persons retiring in Malta among which are 15% flat rate of income tax. No death duties. Free medical and health. Low cost of living. English speaking friendly people. Low crime rate. Reasonably priced properties. Superb climate and located in the heart of the Mediterranean just 3 hours away from the UK. Excellent communications with the rest of Europe.

For a booklet giving you full details of residency conditions and taxation and our regular three-monthly newspaper kindly contact our offices.

Our sales department is staffed with a team of sales representatives who have been expertly trained and have gained vast experience in matters dealing with property, including: valuations, negotiations and finalisation of sales in Malta and Gozo.

Head Office: 2 Paceville Avenue, Paceville, St Julians, STJ 06, Malta.
Telephone: (0356) 337273, Facsimile: (0356) 318037.
Paola Branch: 171, Cospicua Road, Paola, PLA 07, Malta.
Telephone: (0356) 662417, Facsimile: (0356) 697204.
Gozo Branch: 15, Fortunato Mizzi Street, Victoria, VCT 111, Gozo.
Telephone: (0356) 560169, 560170. Facsimile: (0356) 552772.

ESTABLISHED 1969
FRANK SALT
REAL ESTATE LIMITED

ONE NAME PROVIDES ALL YOUR INSURANCE NEEDS.

COPELAND INSURANCE

0181 656 8435
Fax: 0181 655 1271

230/234 Portland Road
London SE25 4SL

EUROPLAN Overseas Property Insurance- A policy that fully protects your overseas property with a UK plan underwritten at Lloyd's. The policy includes cover when the property is left unoccupied for long periods or sublet to tenants. *Immediate quotes *Fast documentation *Very competitive premiums *English policy wording *Premium payment in sterling *Prompt claim settlement.

HEALTHCARE
The best value expatriate medical insurance around today. The most comprehensive cover at the most competitive rates. Free choice of doctors and hospitals, including repatriation to your home country and 24 hour, all year round, multi-lingual emergency medical assistance line.

MOTORCARE
* 12 month Green Card allows year round European motoring.
* Full comprehensive cover available at very competitive rates.
* PLUS, for foreign registered vehicles; accidental damage, fire and theft cover to complement your locally insured third

PROPERTY PROTECTION
* A policy designed to insure UK properties that remain unoccupied for long periods whilst you are away.

HOW TO BUY YOUR DREAM HOME IN SPAIN OR PORTUGAL, IN ENGLISH.

For Spain and Portugal, including the Canaries and Balearics, we've got the experience and range of mortgages to make buying a property easier – with no language barriers and no legal or currency confusion.

For mortgages in plain, simple English call Abbey National Gibraltar Ltd on

(00) 350 76090

OFFSHORE

Abbey National Offshore is a registered business name of Abbey National (Gibraltar) Ltd. Abbey National (Gibraltar) Ltd is licensed by the Gibraltar Financial Service Commission. Licence Number FSC 00044B. Abbey National (Gibraltar) Ltd will require a charge over the property and a life assurance policy may also be required. Loans are subject to status and valuation and are not available to persons under 18. Written quotations available on request. Abbey National plc, Baker St, London NW1 6XL, United Kingdom.

YOUR HOME IS AT RISK IF YOU DO NOT KEEP UP REPAYMENTS ON A MORTGAGE OR OTHER LOAN SECURED ON IT. THE STERLING EQUIVALENT OF YOUR LIABILITY UNDER A FOREIGN CURRENCY MORTGAGE MAY BE INCREASED BY EXCHANGE RATE MOVEMENTS.

Please complete and send to: Abbey National Gibraltar, 7 Main Street, P.O. Box 8, Gibraltar.

NAME:_____

ADDRESS:_____

_____COUNTRY OF INTEREST:_____

Introduction

As more and more of us go overseas on holiday — and with increasing frequency — it is not surprising that we are seduced by the life we see. The easy pace, the warm climate, sun, sea and sand, olive groves and vineyards, afternoons spent drinking the local wine in a Continental cafe, eating alfresco and often at a fraction of the cost at home.

But committing yourself to buying a home overseas or even living there is a far cry from just visiting. Millions of Brits may think to themselves 'wouldn't it be wonderful to spend the rest of my years here in paradise, or even every holiday or summer'. But often, turning your dream into reality without the nightmares suffered by others is a long, tedious and expensive process.

It is nowhere near as simple as buying a home in the UK, and not just because of language and cultural differences.

You may be thinking to yourself: 'I could easily afford a holiday home in Spain/France/Portugal' (or wherever you dream of spending your time). 'After all, I can always make money renting it out as a holiday let. It will finance itself. And if I don't like it, I can always sell up and get my money back.' What a dream. And it is one many of us have shared, particularly on cold, damp days as we trudge to work on the train or as we fly back to Britain from holiday. And why not?

Buying a home abroad can fulfil all your dreams. It can be affordable. An overseas home can make us money. And we can make a profit. *But not always.* For many buying a home overseas can prove to be a nightmare instead of the perfect dream. Prices can plummet, legal problems can mean that you are faced with a massive bill or — worse — you could find that you do not really own the home you have spent your life savings buying. You can be lumbered with massive maintenance bills, huge tax liabilities or even be stranded overseas while ill and with no means to get home.

This book is designed to help you prevent such nightmares. Just as with buying a home at home, you should take your time and go through the usual legal checks, evaluate your finances and look at all aspects of your new home, from transport to hospital and education facilities to future planning proposals. You are unlikely to be familiar with the different tax and legal regimes overseas even if you do know the language. And most importantly you must decide whether you really want to make such a commitment. It is not unknown for those moving abroad to come back within a few months because they cannot cope with the isolation of living in a foreign country, the language problems or even the cost of living there.

Even if you are only buying a property to enjoy for a few months of the year, you must take into account the fact that you will then be tied to one place for your holidays. Will you get fed up visiting the same place year after year?

So before reading the chapter on the country of your choice, read Part I of the book. That way you will not be seduced into making a wrong decision.

Part I
General Guidelines on Buying a Property Abroad

1
Is buying a property overseas the right thing for me?

This may sound an obvious and somewhat silly question, but *why* do you want to buy a home overseas? As you have started to read this book, you will probably have a good idea of the answer. But make sure you have really thought out your reasons for taking such a step. Remember, buying a home overseas can be a costly and lengthy process and, as the recent residential property price slump across most world markets has proved, it can leave you nursing serious losses. However, demand is increasing again and this, combined with comparatively low prices, means that now is possibly the ideal time to buy.

Even if you are retiring or going to live or work abroad, you do not have to buy immediately. It is often best to try before you buy — that way you will be sure that you really know what you are letting yourself in for.

It may sound negative, but in some cases you may be better off not buying at all as the outgoings on your property — not just initially but year after year — could finance luxury holidays for the rest of your life.

However, nothing can beat the feeling of having your own home, somewhere you love to retreat to, with familiar surroundings, the kitchen, bathroom and furniture you want, the garden or view you have always dreamed of and a place you can be proud of and invite your friends to visit.

Ask yourself the following questions:

- Can I really afford to buy overseas? This is not just a question of raising the finance or spending your savings, but also the extra cost of buying which is often at least 10 per cent of the purchase

price as well as the ongoing maintenance costs and bills. And you will have to remember the costs of getting there and back on a regular basis.
- Is it best to buy? Even if you are planning to live abroad on a permanent basis, do you really need to buy a home overseas? Britain has one of the highest levels of home ownership in the world and as such we automatically tend to think that buying is the best way of providing ourselves and our families with a home. But you should also consider renting — even if only on a short-term basis — to ensure you are making the right decision. (See Chapter 3 for alternatives.)
- Do I really like the country and the people? This is often overlooked, particularly by those who are seduced into buying overseas after a few brief visits. You may find that you hate the slow pace of life that you loved so much when you were on holiday. If you cannot get anything done — from fixing the plumbing to connecting the phone — without months of hassle and delay you can quickly learn to hate the country. And it is no good moving to a country where you dislike the local people, for example if you think all Americans are brash or you dislike the French as much as they sometimes seem to dislike us. And don't forget the climate. Living in a hot country may seem tempting after a British winter, but can you really cope with stifling heat week in week out?
- Am I prepared to learn the local language? You may not need to speak it fluently but you should be prepared to learn at least a little. Remember, as a homeowner you will not only be dealing with shop assistants and bartenders who may speak good English, but also plumbers, motor mechanics and decorators who may not. Remember, you *are* the foreigner and will be treated as such.
- Could I cope with being ill abroad? If you are planning to travel regularly to a particular country or live there on a permanent basis, you must bear in mind that your good health cannot be guaranteed. As the saying goes accidents can happen and if the worst comes to the worst, are the medical facilities of a high enough standard?
- Can I cope with and do I have time for all the hassle? Owning any home involves paperwork, bills, maintenance and repairs. Overseas these everyday chores can turn into major projects. In some countries you have to pay bills in person and, if you do not

settle them on time, suffer financial penalties and disconnection. When you buy a holiday home remember it has to be looked after all year round, not just when you visit. Even if you appoint a local representative to keep an eye on your home, you will still be involved in a substantial amount of paperwork yourself.

- Can I afford to lose financially? Although property prices are stabilised and are now rising in most of the popular locations for second/holiday homes, bear in mind the experiences of those who purchased homes overseas in the 1980s. Some of them have lost up to half the value of their property. Exchange fluctuations, tax changes, new planning and building legislation, a decline in the popularity of the resort or town and the state of the local economy can all impact on property prices. That means a repeat experience of the property slump cannot be ruled out in the future. Remember property prices can go down as well as up.
- Am I prepared to integrate? One of the things most Brits miss when living overseas — even if only for a few weeks at a time — is the television and certain foods. It may seem strange that we miss British food in France but it is amazing how many people take baked beans with them. Satellite TV gets round the yearning for English speaking programmes in many countries. And there are the other considerations such as the neighbours — a problem enough for many at home — and the other idiosyncracies such as restaurants and bars that close just when you want to go and eat or shops that are not open at times that suit you.
- Will my family be happy? If you are taking children you must consider how they will fit in, particularly if you want to educate them overseas. If they dislike the place you could find that instead of your dream of spending evenings enjoying a feast on the patio with a noisy group of family and friends, you are spending evenings quietly alone wondering why nobody wants to visit.

2
Can I really afford to buy a property abroad?

Cheaper property prices on the Continent and in America are one of the major attractions of buying a home overseas. When you hear of unmodernised French farmhouses on sale for £20,000, substantial bungalows in Florida on a complex complete with golf course and swimming pool for £60,000 and studio flats in Tenerife for just £18,000 it seems that you cannot lose if you buy.

But before you swap your three-bedroomed semi in suburbia for a sprawling villa overlooking the sea or go out to raise a second mortgage, remember the costs do not end there.

These are the extra costs you must take into account:

- Buying a property in Britain can be relatively cheap. Purchasing costs overseas can easily add a further 10 or 20 per cent to the purchase price. There will usually be legal fees, land registry charges, purchase taxes and money transfer fees.
- Local taxes and rates — these will come out of your income. So even if you can afford to buy the property out of savings or with a mortgage, you will also have to find extra income to cover them.
- Removal costs — even if you are only buying a home for holidays you may find it cheaper to move extra furniture from Britain than to buy overseas.
- Maintenance — every property needs maintenance. Even if you are purchasing a flat there will be a service charge.
- Insurance. What would you do if your dream home was struck by lightning? Or if the contents were stolen? If the home is empty for much of the year, premiums are likely to be much higher.
- Accountancy fees — many countries require foreign nationals to submit a tax return even if they only own a holiday home.

- Local representative — this is a must if you leave your home unoccupied for any length of time. You don't want your services cut off because you were not there when the bill and final reminder arrived. A local agent is also advisable if you are letting out your property (for more details see Chapter 4).
- Getting there — flights or ferry tickets can be expensive, particularly in peak season.
- Inflation and exchange rates — just because you can afford to live abroad or run a property overseas today, does not mean you will in the future. If your income is in sterling and exchange rates fluctuate even by a small amount, could you really cope with a 5 or even 20 per cent reduction in your income? Britain now has a very low inflation rate so the threat of rising prices is often ignored. But elsewhere inflation rates can be a serious threat. If prices are rising rapidly you can quickly discover that although you can afford to pay for the property you cannot afford to run it or that your enjoyment suffers because prices in shops and restaurants have risen so much.

Raising the capital required

There are several ways of financing the actual property purchase.

Savings

You may have enough savings built up or a lump sum from your retirement pension to finance the property outright.

Selling your existing home

This is not the ideal solution if you want to return to the UK at a later stage. A couple of years ago, who would have thought this was a problem? But the recent surge in property prices has proved that it is not worth gambling on the fact that you will be able to afford the same type of home that you sold when you moved abroad. If price rises continue at their current rate, in a decade many of those living abroad may find that they cannot afford to return home because house prices are out of their financial reach. The alternative is to sell your home here and buy a smaller one in the UK which you can then rent out or use as a second home and then use the capital released by the sale to purchase your overseas property. Or you can simply rent out your UK home and use the income to fund a mortgage on your overseas property.

Raising a second mortgage on your existing home

This can be done only if you have sufficient equity (the difference between the amount you owe on your home loan and the value of the property) and enough income. Lenders will want security for their loan so you will not be able to borrow against your existing property if you have a 100 per cent mortgage. If you are borrowing from a UK lender you can usually raise up to two and a half times your annual income less the amount of any other mortgage. Mortgages for the purchase of overseas homes do not qualify for mortgage interest tax relief.

Taking out a loan

You can take out an unsecured loan if you do not require a large sum, say not much more than £10,000, provided you have enough income (and a good credit record) to qualify. But remember the interest rates will be higher than those on a mortgage.

Raising a mortgage on your overseas property

This will use the overseas home — not your home in the UK — as security. As such you should go to a UK mortgage adviser that specialises in this area or to a bank in the country where you want to purchase your property. This will help to overcome valuation problems and to smooth the path when it comes to transferring money. Try to pick a bank which has links with a UK bank or is a subsidiary of one. The larger banks in most of the countries favoured by Brits are usually prepared to lend to foreign nationals but you may only be able to borrow half of the property value. Remember exchange fluctuations. If your income is in sterling it may be better for you to borrow in sterling. Your decision should take into account the interest rates in the country where you are buying, the stability of the currency and the lending terms. In some countries you may qualify for tax relief if you borrow from a bank in that country and if you let out your property abroad, you may be able to claim interest costs against your UK tax liability.

Loaning from the developer

If you are planning to buy a new property the developer may have already arranged finance. This can make life easier for you, but check that you are not being charged an excessively high interest rate and that there are no hidden catches.

3
Alternative ways to buy a home overseas

As with the British property market, there are more ways to owning a home abroad than buying a freehold. At home you can buy a leasehold and a timeshare as well as the more traditional route of buying a property outright.

Each type of purchase can have its benefits and disadvantages. The most obvious is cost. This chapter looks at the various options to help you keep an open mind when looking for a home overseas.

Long-term renting

Ok, this is *not* owning a home overseas. But it *is* a way to get into the property market in a foreign country before commiting yourself to a long-term purchase. Renting, at least in the short term, is advisable before making a long-term commitment.

Remember to apply the same judgements when buying abroad as you would at home. How will property values hold up, what is the neighbourhood like, how good are the transport, health and education facilities, what are the local people like and will I/we fit in, will I feel at home here and numerous other questions. That is why renting (for more than just a summer or holiday period) is highly advisable. After all, would you move across Britain for a new job and buy on the spot? Most people would check out the best places to buy and work out if that is really where they want to live before committing themselves to a purchase. Do the same when buying overseas.

Condominiums

This is a strange concept to most Brits who are used to buying flats on a leasehold basis. In America and on the Continent most apartments — and sometimes even houses — are sold on this basis. Unlike the leasehold system the purchaser does not buy the property for a set term but owns their property outright. There are rules covering the management of the block of flats and communal areas, the election of residents to this management committee and also rules governing what you can and cannot do with your property. You will have to pay a service fee to cover your share of the costs.

The advantage of this system is that you do not have to hand the property back when the lease term ends and you do not run the risk of having to cope with a 'shark' landlord who fails to maintain the building. But running a building on a condominium basis can also have problems, particularly if the residents cannot agree — see individual country chapters for more details.

Timeshare

Again this is a concept that you are unlikely to consider when buying in your home country. And you may not want to consider it abroad either. The timeshare concept has suffered from much adverse publicity, but this does not mean that it is always a bad idea. Buying a timeshare can work in your favour if you cannot afford to buy a property outright and do not want the bother of paying someone to look after your holiday home when it is unoccupied. The Timeshare Council at 22 Buckingham Gate, London SW1E 6LB (Tel 0171–821 8845) provides useful information for those considering this as an option.

> **Warning**
>
> Consumer protection for those buying timeshares varies from country to country so investigate your rights before signing anything.

Timeshare is the right to occupy and use a property, usually a furnished apartment, villa or hotel suite by purchasing selected, specific weeks or weeks in a specified seasonal time band annually, for a contracted number of years. You buy the timeshare outright at the start. In addition you pay an annual charge to cover maintenance and management. This charge can, and will, rise so be prepared for increasing costs.

You will usually have the right to exchange, let or sell your timeshare. This means that you can experience other countries and resorts.

Timeshare is a big business. There are now 3.5 million timeshare owners in over 4500 resorts around the world. Do not allow yourself to be pressurised into buying a timeshare as not all countries allow you a 'cooling-off' period in which to cancel and get a refund. Always get a full description of your timeshare showing your legal ownership rights and details and where possible contact the owners' committee.

Freehold

If you are not buying an apartment or house on a purpose-built complex then you are likely to be buying your property on a freehold basis. Just as in the UK you should get your solicitor to check that the property is free from mortgages and other debts or that these are settled upon purchase, that there are no rights of way affecting the property and that all planning requirements have been met.

4
What you need to know about buying a second/holiday home

Buying a property that you are not going to occupy all of the time comes with its own set of problems.

Just as you would feel uncomfortable about leaving your home in the UK empty for weeks or even months on end so you should about a home overseas. At home you may have a friendly neighbour or relative who lives nearby to keep an eye on your property. But overseas you may not.

That is why it is essential to employ someone to look after your overseas home when you are not there.

This problem can be solved by living in an apartment block with a resident caretaker whom you could ask to keep an eye on your flat and forward your post. A small payment or bottle of whisky is likely to win some goodwill. On holiday home complexes there may also be a caretaker who can help you or the manager of the residents' committee may be able to offer some advice.

If you are required to file a local income tax return it will probably be worth your while to employ an accountant. Even if you have only small amounts of tax to pay, language problems can mean that you suffer. And remember, not every country has as efficient a banking system as the UK. You may not be able to pay bills by direct debit or standing order and in some countries you are required to pay your bill in person. If you are not there when the bill arrives and fail to get the final reminder you could return to your holiday home and find that you have no power and no telephone and face a hefty bill for reconnection.

Of course, if you can afford it, a housekeeper can avoid many of these problems. If you have a substantial property with swimming pool and gardens, a caretaker may also be a wise investment, even if only to prevent deterioration of the property which will save on major bills in the long run.

And lastly do not forget tax. You may be liable for capital gains tax when you come to sell.

Renting out your holiday home

Many of those who own a second home abroad help to finance this by letting it out. There are several ways of doing this.

Renting out to friends, relatives and colleagues

This is one way to ensure that your tenants look after your home and if they do not at least you will know how to get hold of them. If you know enough people to rent to and that provides sufficient income for your requirements then this will be the safest option. It is also the cheapest as you do not have to pay an agent to let them into the property and to read meters and there are no advertising costs. However, you may not be able to get away with charging so much rent.

Renting to British holidaymakers

By advertising in the UK for tenants you can interview them and take a deposit in advance as well as references. However, you will still need to employ someone to let the tenants in, to clean the property before they arrive, read the meters and collect any post.

You can advertise your property in newspapers or in magazines such as *The Lady*. Remember, where you advertise is important, particularly if you want to attract a certain type of tenant or your home will only appeal to a particular group of people. There is no point in advertising a studio flat in a noisy resort in a publication that is read by affluent families looking for large, remote villas.

Register your property with an agent overseas

This could mean that you have tenants from all over the globe. But it is up to the agent to find them and to oversee cleaning, taking of deposits and meter reading. You will have to pay for this service and before signing up make sure that you are dealing with a reputable company. If your tenants do not get their deposits returned they may come to you for redress. Alternatively your agent may fail to ensure that the property is kept in good order, may fail to keep an inventory or may not pass on the full amount of cash you are due.

24 / Buying Abroad: General Guidelines

Register your property with a travel firm

This will only apply to particularly desirable properties and often you are required to ensure that the tenants are given the keys, that the property is clean and that everything is in working order. This will be difficult if you are in the UK. However, if you are included in a travel firm's brochure you are likely to get a good rate of occupancy. Remember, the rent that is advertised will not be all yours – the travel firm is in business to make money and will charge for your property appearing in its glossy brochure.

Renting out rooms

You could offer a bed and breakfast type service. However, the low cost of package holidays means that most holidaymakers can afford to stay in hotels so you may find that there is little demand. If your property is in an area where there are few hotels and demand is high — for instance in rural Provence — you could make a tidy income. And do not forget that you will have to pay tax on this income.

Tips

If you are letting out your holiday home bear the following points in mind:

- Ask tenants to bring their own linen to save on laundry bills.
- Don't forget to take an inventory and do not leave valuables around the home.
- If you are letting out the property to strangers, do not buy expensive furnishings or items that can be easily damaged.
- If you have a phone line consider installing a pay phone or one that only accepts incoming calls to prevent a stranger running up a massive phone bill.
- Always ensure that the property is clean and tidy before holidaymakers arrive.
- Don't make claims that are not true. You could get into trouble if they ask for the money back or threaten to sue.
- Remember, your reputation is very important. If you can get repeat business from reliable tenants it will ensure that your property is regularly let and you will save on the cost of advertising for new holidaymakers.

- Reserve some weeks for yourself. There is no point in buying a holiday home if you cannot enjoy it.
- Don't rely on rental income to finance the purchase of the property. You may not be able to get a high enough rent (check with local agents before buying) and may not be able to get enough customers.
- If you have bought a flat in a condominium check the terms of your purchase as there may be restrictions on letting out the property.
- Always ask customers to sign a formal agreement if you are arranging the letting yourself. If you are using an agent he or she should have a form for tenants to sign. And remember the laws of the country you are letting in will apply so seek legal advice to avoid any pitfalls.
- Keep a record of all costs involved in letting the property for tax purposes.
- Try to visit your property when a holidaymaker is there so that you can check that all your arrangements are in order, your agent/cleaner/maintenance person is doing his or her job and to get feedback from the customer. You may not have noticed a problem with your home that they have and you may get some useful tips to improve the stay of other tenants.

5
Retiring abroad

This is one of the most common reasons for buying a home overseas and even some younger buyers who have bought a home for holiday purposes only do so with a view to retiring to their overseas home in the long term.

The obvious appeal of retiring overseas is the weather which can help alleviate many of the ailments associated with ageing as well as making a future life of leisure more enjoyable.

An estimated 750,000 pensioners live in foreign countries. For many, retirement means a cash lump sum and freedom from commitments, allowing them to fulfil their dreams of living overseas.

Pensions and income

Retirement usually means a large drop in income and even if you are in receipt of a substantial pension it may not keep pace with inflation in the country you choose to make your home. Even if you have substantial capital in addition to the money you have used to buy your home overseas, there is no guarantee that this will provide sufficient income or last the 20 or more years of your retirement.

This can be a major problem if you are stuck overseas with rising living costs plus medical and other bills and an income which is dwindling in real terms. You must take this possibility into account.

State pensions

Retired people entitled to a state pension will be paid this in the country they have moved to as long as they let the DSS know where they are living. Each year thousands of people fail to claim the pensions due to them. However, if you are about to retire you do not have to claim your pension immediately if you do not need it. When you do come to claim it may be increased to reflect this deferment.

Both state and occupational pensions are liable to UK tax — but check the relevant double taxation agreement which will ensure that if you pay tax in an overseas country you are not charged a second time in the UK.

Before leaving Britain ask for Form 121 from the Department of Social Security (see below for address) and this will be sent to the appropriate social security authority in the country you are planning to live in and will certify that you are entitled to a pension.

Health facilities

Good medical facilities are a must for anyone retiring overseas as there is a greater chance that you will need to use them.

Pensioners living in EC countries are entitled to claim medical and health facilities that are available to nationals of the country concerned. Benefits include free dental treatment, sickness benefit and often free drugs.

However, you may not want to rely on local facilities. Before leaving Britain check out your entitlements by requesting *Your Social Security, Health Care and Pension Rights in the European Community* (Form SA29), from your local Social Security Office or direct from the DSS Overseas Branch, Newcastle upon Tyne NE98 1YX.

If you are retiring outside the EC, you will need private health insurance (a must in the US). However, for a pensioner this can be very expensive and you should budget for this before even contemplating going to live abroad. A typical scheme for someone over retirement age can cost anything from £1000 to £2600 a year. You may be able to cut these costs but only at the expense of cover.

Climate

You may be retiring overseas for no other reason than the weather — but remember, living in 90° Fahrenheit heat on a permanent basis is nothing like enjoying it for two weeks at a time when you visit on holiday. And don't forget to consider what the weather is like in winter. Some coastal resorts can suffer from high winds.

Security

Again this is important for older people retiring abroad. They may still feel as vulnerable as they do at home. Try to avoid buying in a busy holiday complex which becomes deserted in winter or anywhere that is too remote (however fit and well you are today).

Social life

Although the last people you may want to mix with when you move abroad are other 'expats' who have gone there to retire, it is not a bad thing to keep in with the local British community. You never know when you might need to hear a friendly English voice. Loneliness can be a major problem for those retiring thousands of miles away from friends and family. However, you are likely to find that you get many requests to visit by people looking for a cheap holiday.

Other facilities

You should also ensure that there are enough shopping and transport facilities as well as plenty of social or sporting clubs, a nearby bank, post office and an English-speaking doctor if possible. You may be fit and well now, but consider how you would cope with even mundane tasks such as shopping if you lost your mobility or fell ill.

Death of a partner

The problems you must be prepared to face are not only isolation, loneliness, the possibility of a reduced income and sickness but also bereavement. This, sadly, is more common than you may think. A couple retire abroad to enjoy their autumn years in the sun and one of them passes away. The other is left to sort out the burial, registration of the death, legal requirements, inheritance or death duties and the will. They are also left alone and may find it hard to sell the property in order to return home. It is not a pleasant thought, but you should bear this possibility in mind.

6
Taking your children with you

For some of you, moving overseas means the chance to start a whole new life. You are not just looking for a holiday home or a place to retire, but are planning to work there for several years or even permanently.

If you have children of school age there will be special considerations.

Education

You have several options:

- educate your children at a boarding school in the UK;
- educate them at an international or English school in the country you are moving to; or
- educate them at a local school.

A lot will depend on the age of your children. If they are young enough to go through the entire education system of the country you are planning to move to they will probably learn the new language easily and quickly fit in. They will then become bilingual. Of course, you may not consider the local education system to be of a high enough standard. But there are advantages in sending your child to a local school where they can meet friends and integrate into the community.

Older children, who are nearing examinations, will probably be better off at a boarding school in the UK or a good English-speaking school overseas that offers the same examinations.

Sending your children to a boarding school is expensive (unless the firm you work for is prepared to foot the bill) and you will only see your children at half-term and holidays. However, moving your children overseas when they are already halfway through their education at home can be traumatic. If they are near to completing their exams it may be unwise to move them.

If you have parents, relatives or close friends living near your existing home it may be better to leave your children in their care so that your children do not have to suffer the upheaval of moving school and leaving their friends at such a critical time in their education.

But remember, children are often more adaptable than adults and usually find it easier to learn a second language. Living overseas is often a way to ensure that you children are bi- or even trilingual — a major asset in future life.

If you are working in the EU your children will probably be entitled to free education.

7
Practical problems in moving

Moving is one of the most stressful events in life along with death of a loved one, redundancy and divorce. So imagine the stress levels when you are not moving across town but across the world. Even if you are only planning to buy a home for holidays you will have to consider moving some items of furniture and personal belongings overseas. Moving lock, stock and barrel will be even more traumatic.

These are the things to consider:

- *How much should I take?* This is difficult and may depend on how cheap furniture is where you are moving to and how attached you are to your existing possessions.
- *How do prices compare?* Always check out the competition. There are several reputable international removers who will give you quotes — and often advice. You must also add on the costs of insuring your belongings while they are in store and in transit.
- *Will they deliver to the door?* Some freight forwarding agents will only deliver as far as the port of entry of the destination country. This means that it is up to you to arrange customs clearance and transfer to your new home.
- *Will I need to find storage?* If you do not want to take everything with you and are not keeping a base in the UK you will have to store your belongings which can be expensive. And remember, the legal process in some countries is very slow. So you may uproot only to find the sale has not been finalised and you will again need to find storage.
- *Will I be able to take electrical items?* These may not be compatible with voltages overseas and your TV and video will probably not work in your new country.
- *Will I have to pay import duty on my belongings?* There may be a small customs clearance fee but it is unlikely that you will be

charged VAT if you are only taking personal items into another country. You are allowed to buy certain goods free of VAT charges in the UK if you are intending to spend at least 12 months out of the country. Check with your remover and local tax office for details.

- *What about my car?* You will probably escape VAT in the import of this provided you (or rather the garage) have paid it here in the UK. But not all countries allow you to import cars and when they do you will have to comply with the legislation of that country. So if you have an old car without the correct catalytic converter or other safety measures this could be difficult. If you are taking a new car abroad you can buy it without the payment of VAT in the UK. This will have to be cleared by Customs and Excise and can be done by filling in form 411 (for motor exports to another EEC country — details are explained in notice 728) or form 410 (if exporting outside the EEC — details in notice 705). Contact your local Customs and Excise Office for information and forms. Check that you are then not liable for tax upon import of the car overseas and the penalties you will face if you bring the car back into the UK.

   Do not forget to check out the local requirements on MOTs, insurance, safety belts, road tax, your driving licence and other safety factors as well as the rules of the road.

   If you take your existing car abroad for longer than 12 months you will have to contact your local Vehicle Licensing Office as it will be regarded as a permanent export.

   There are also practical problems to consider. After a lifetime of driving on the left, you will probably have to drive on the 'wrong' side of the road. You may find it easier to do this with a right-hand drive than by converting to a left-hand drive vehicle, therefore you may be better off taking your existing car with you. But if it is a British car or there is no local garage specialising in your make of vehicle, you may find it expensive and difficult to get repairs and maintenance done.

- *What about my pet?* You may find it possible to take your pet with you, but you will find it difficult to bring your cat or dog back again. Britain still has quarantine laws although there is increasing pressure for these to be reformed and replaced by pet 'passports' detailing vaccinations and confirming that your pet is disease free.

You should also have your pets vaccinated to protect them from diseases (particularly rabies) they may contract in the country where you are planning to live.

Regulations vary from country to country. Taking your pet to France will require an export health certificate. Form EXA1 is obtainable from the Ministry of Agriculture, Fisheries and Food (MAFF), Hook Rise South, Surbiton, Surrey, KT6 7NF. When this is completed send it to your local Animal Health Office who will then pass it on to your local veterinary inspector for completion. No import permit is required for Greece, Spain or Italy but again a local veterinary inspector of MAFF will be required to provide a certificate. However, rules vary: some countries require MAFF export certificates to be issued 14 days before export and others two days. In other European countries such as Portugal import permits are required. And most countries require that pets receive vaccinations — although the range of these will vary.

- *Is the removal firm reliable?* Check that the firm has proper backing. You do not want the firm to go bust half way through your move. The British Association of Removers (BAR) has an Overseas Group. There is also the Federation of International Furniture Removers (FIDI) which international member companies of BAR have links with. Membership of FIDI means that a contractor can arrange a door-to-door international removal. A firm in the country of destination will therefore be able to deal with customs clearance, storage (where necessary) and delivery to your new address. BAR also has a guarantee scheme.

The British Association of Removers has a free leaflet. Send a stamped, self-addressed envelope to 3 Churchill Court, 58 Station Road, North Harrow, HA2 7SA.

8
Who you need to tell

There is a vast amount of paperwork involved in moving overseas.

Make sure you arrange a UK contact address as well as one overseas. In addition, a number of organisations must be informed if you are planning to leave the country on a permanent basis.

Financial contacts and professional advisers

These will include your bank, building society, credit card issuer, other lender, investment or financial adviser, solicitor, accountant, the share register of companies you own shares in, insurance companies including life insurer, pension provider or pension scheme and savings organisations.

Suppliers of services

Examples are gas and electricity boards and your local authority.

The Inland Revenue

Tell your income tax office where you are planning to move to and when. And ask them for advice. They have several useful leaflets and can be very helpful.

For details of your tax office see your tax return or the local phone book. (Your tax office may not be in the same town or city as the one in which you live.)

The Department of Social Security

This is not only necessary so that you can arrange pensions/benefits overseas but also so that you do not lose out while you are abroad. The DSS covers benefits, national insurance (NI) and pensions. It will need to know your full name, date of birth and NI number as well as where you are moving to and for how long. Contact the DSS Overseas Branch, Newcastle upon Tyne, NE98 1YX.

Vehicle Licensing Centre

If you are planning to take your car abroad for more than a year you should fill in the permanent export section of your registration document and send it to the Vehicle Licensing Centre, Swansea, SA99 1AB. You should be able to retain your British driving licence in the EC and most other countries. Check before leaving as you may require an international driving licence (contact the AA for advice) or may be required to hold a local driving licence.

Dentist, doctor and optician

It may also be a good idea to stock up on prescriptions before you go. You will also have to contact your local Family Practitioners' Committee.

Post office

If you have forgotten to notify anyone of your move, a letter forwarding service will ensure you still get your mail. But you will have to pay a forwarding fee.

9
Making the most of your money — tax, benefits and avoiding expensive pitfalls

Benefits, social security and health care

In the UK we take state help for granted. If we become ill, we can rely on the National Health Service; if we lose our job, claim unemployment benefit; and, if we are old and infirm, qualify for a range of services and benefits.

Even if you are only holidaying abroad you should check in advance what help is available to you — for instance emergency medical treatment. Main post offices have form E111 which tells you how to claim free healthcare abroad and what healthcare is available to UK citizens.

Moving abroad on a permanent basis you should make sure that you are not missing out on any of your entitlements at home (your UK pension). Within the EC you should qualify for many of the state benefits you would get at home. For instance, if you move to another European country and your son or daughter wants to come with you to look for work, he or she may qualify for unemployment benefit for up to three months. However, if you are in receipt of attendance allowance you are unlikely to qualify for this if you go to live in another EC country. Pensioners should pay particular attention to their entitlements. For instance, if your husband dies when you are living in one EC country, but he was insured in another, you may be able to claim widow's benefits in either of the countries. If you go to work or are self-employed in another EC country you can usually get the children's allowance that country pays — even if your children stay in the UK. The golden rule is to check with the Benefits Agency and the Contributions Agency, both part of the Department of Social Security, before you go.

Offshore companies and trusts

These can both offer tax advantages and can be used when purchasing your property abroad. However, they are likely to appeal only to the very wealthy partly because of the costs of setting them up and the alternative ways to reduce tax available to the average family. (For instance, the first £215,000 of an estate is free from inheritance tax in the UK and, if your assets are not going to exceed this limit, there may be little point in setting up an elaborate scheme to get round a tax you do not have to pay anyway.) Also, remember that in some countries, such as Malta, it is not possible to purchase a property through the use of an offshore company.

Offshore companies are subject to no tax or low rates of tax on income and capital gains. The use of an offshore company enables you to pass your assets on to a next of kin in a discreet and tax-efficient manner as inheritance tax can be avoided. It is possible to incorporate a company in Gibraltar within a matter of days. An exempt company, owned by a non-resident, cannot transact business within Gibraltar (except with other exempt companies) and provided certain conditions are met, will not be liable to pay any form of Gibraltar tax for 25 years. A small fee (currently £200) is paid in lieu of tax.

Trusts set up in the UK are subject to both income and capital gains tax. However, there can be substantial benefits when they are used for inheritance tax planning. Trusts can be located in any country that recognises the trust concept and, as such, no income tax need be paid on the trust income. However, a UK resident trustee will still pay basic rate tax on any trust income.

Income tax, double taxation and domicile

You may think that owning a home in another country is simple in terms of tax. But remember, even if you do not receive any income from your home abroad you may still have to comply with local tax law. For instance, until 1993, all non-residents with an economic interest in Spain had to appoint a fiscal representative or face a fine. Although this rule has now been relaxed it is still advisable to appoint one as even non-residents should pay the wealth tax on the value of their property and a nominal 2 per cent of their property value as income tax. The same applies in France where non-residents must pay tax on ownership of property even if they receive no rental income. UK citizens should be able to avoid this, but again, it is important to assess tax liabilities before purchase.

Becoming domiciled in another country — particularly one with lower tax rates than apply in the UK — can have its advantages. Generally, you will have to buy a property in your new country, make a will under its law, apply for permanent residency (if not nationality), dispose of your UK residence, close UK bank accounts and open ones in your new country and take steps to prove that you are a permanent resident in your new country. Domicile is often described as the country which you regard as your homeland and one where you intend to die. That is why an immigrant is sometimes advised to buy a burial plot!

You are allowed to visit England for up to 90 days a year while retaining your new domicile. Or vice versa, if you spend more than 182 days in any tax year in your new country or have a habitual residence, you will have to pay tax on your world-wide income in that country. So, even though you may not be domiciled there for tax, you may be resident there for tax and as such will have to pay income tax in that country on your world-wide income. In this case, the double taxation treaty that the UK has with most other countries should ensure that you are not taxed twice — in the UK and your new place of residency. You will probably be taxed in the country in which you have your closest association. If this is another country, you can apply to the Inland Revenue Foreign Intermediaries Claims Office to enable these payments to be made without deduction of UK tax.

Wills

Although an English will is acceptable and recognised in most other countries, it is always advisable to make a separate will in the country where you are buying your overseas home, covering assets held in that country. The will should meet that country's legal requirements and not conflict with your UK will; tell your solicitor so that he does not automatically include wording to the effect that the will revokes all previous wills. And make clear in your overseas will that it covers only your assets in that country. Particular attention should be paid to different legal systems. For instance, if you have become domiciled in

France but have a UK will, your assets may be distributed according to French law — which offers little protection for your spouse, as most of your assets must be passed on to your children.

Inheritance tax/succession tax rates vary from country to country. Although tax rates may be lower elsewhere, you can reduce your tax liability in the UK (and even eliminate it completely) by careful tax planning. If you are planning to be domiciled for tax purposes in another country, check the rates of inheritance tax as well as the more obvious income tax rates. This may make you think twice about domicile. For instance, in France there is no exemption on assets left to a spouse (unlike in the UK).

Part II
A Country-by-Country Guide to Buying Your Property Abroad

Buying a home in Spain

To many of us who holiday in Spain, it is a land of sun, sea, sand and sangria and siestas on hot afternoons. No wonder it not only remains a favourite holiday destination, with over six million of us visiting every year, but it is also the most popular location with the British for buying a foreign home. There are some quarter of a million British subjects living in Spain, mostly on the Mediterranean coast. And some one million properties are owned by foreigners. What makes it so attractive?

For a start there is 1317 miles of coastline with over 700 miles of this along the Mediterranean to the south and east and over 600 on the Atlantic to the west. In addition to mainland Spain there are the Balearic islands — such as Minorca and Majorca — as well as the Canaries. Flights are relatively cheap and there are plenty of airports. The climate is good all year round with 300–320 days of sun a year over the Mediterranean costas and the islands. And the property prices are cheap compared with Britain. Although the cost of living is now about the same as Britain (so it is no longer cheaper to live there), the warm weather means you can save on heating and heavy clothing.

But Spain is more than just beaches and holiday resorts and there are arguments for living slightly away from the tourist hotspots if you want to make more of a permanent home there. For a start prices are cheaper without the tourist mark-up and you will also get to know a bit more of the real Spain.

Spain is still a patchwork of separate 'countries' stitched together just a few centuries ago. Its system of regional governments recognises this historical need for local autonomy. Catalonia and the Costa Brava are very different from Andalucia and the Costa del Sol. The seven Canary Islands are actually two regions. The Balearics are also very different from each other.

The property market

The Spanish holiday homes market is very mature and there is no shortage of properties. The fact that so many Britons have bought homes there — either for holiday use or to live in or retire to permanently — means that when you buy a home there you are benefiting from the years of experience others have gained. As a result the pitfalls are well known and you can expect to receive a high level of service from property companies, estate agents and lenders.

Although the Spanish property market is now coming out of the slump suffered across most of Europe from the late 1980s, prices are still well down on their peak in many areas. Bankers there, like bankers here, have put the squeeze on developers after the slump, but there is tangible evidence that the growth of the property market will be sustained. In 1996 there was a resurgence in new construction in the Marbella area, not seen since the 1980s. Property prices bottomed out in early 1995 and have risen steadily but slowly — an increasing volume of sales kept up competition for buyers and as a result price rises were low. Now this surplus has been removed, higher price rises seem assured. The low resale market also means that more new developments are being built to meet increasing demand.

But unlike the late 1980s today's developers are only too aware that the market is now far more sophisticated, demanding higher quality of design and construction.

Detached villas outside the more closely packed holiday estates which afford privacy as well as convenience are showing growing popularity — partly because, unlike a decade or so ago, they come with good paved roads, mains electricity and water supplies and a telephone. So buyers no longer need to seek the security of a large development. As a result country properties now account for some 45 per cent of total property sales up from just 5 per cent a decade ago.

Despite the recent rise in property prices, bargains can still be had, particularly at the bottom end of the market.

However, purchasing a property, owning and reselling have become more complicated for non-residents. Despite the advent of the Single European Market, there is now more legal and taxation red tape than before. But it has also become a safer place in which to invest. The greater bureaucracy involved means that seeking professional advice, particularly from an independent lawyer specialising in this field and from a tax adviser, is strongly recommended.

NOTARIAL and LEGAL SERVICES

M. FLOREZ VALCARCEL

SPANISH LAWYER & NOTARY PUBLIC
("ABOGADO & NOTARIO")

For advice and general assistance regarding Spanish law matters and in particular

SPANISH PROPERTY CONVEYANCING,

winding up of Spanish estates, formation of companies, Wills, Power of Attorney, etc.

TELEPHONE AND FAX: 0181 741 4867
130 KINGS STREET, LONDON W6 0QU.

Where to look

We often forget how large a country Spain is and tend to think of it as a series of holiday resorts. It has a population of almost 40 million and is almost 200,000 square miles in size, making it the second largest European country after France. Spain has a vast coastline as well as many inland regions. Each coast and region is very different — reflecting the fact that Spain is in fact a tapestry of different cultures which often have their own language and traditions.

There are 18 autonomous regions with their own parliaments and governments: Andalucia, Aragon, Asturias, Balearics, Basque country, two regions in the Canaries, Castilla-La Mancha, Castilla-Leon, Cantabria, Catalonia, Estremadura, Galicia, Madrid, Murcia, Navarra, La Rioja and Valencia.

The improving Spanish economy combined with low prices for holiday homes following the property slump, will mean that competition for the best bargains is likely to come from Spanish families from the cities rather than other Brits or expats.

It is advisable to check out any estate agents or property developers you approach. Estate agents should be qualified by examination and registered as well as licensed. Ask them to send you property details on a regular basis so you can judge the type of properties available in the areas you are interested in, the prices and the level of supply and demand.

Before deciding whereabouts in Spain you want to start looking for a property make a check list of the following:

- *Am I familiar with a particular area?* If you are then that is where you are most likely to start looking. But make sure that you *really* know what the place is like. It is impossible to judge from just a few weeks' holiday what the area is like out of season.
- *Do I know other people who live there?* If you do this will be a big plus. It is never easy living away from friends and family and leaving a familiar environment, however nice your new home is. And with language barriers, a friendly British voice — particularly when your friends are not visiting you — will ensure you do not feel isolated and lonely. Even if you are only buying a property for holidays and feel you really want to get away from it all, it does help if there are other Brits living in your area.
- *What is the climate like* and what sort of weather would I feel comfortable with?
- *What are the transport facilities like and how near is it to the airport?* Good access is a big plus if you want to let your property out and you will also find it easier to sell when you decide to move on.
- *Is it too busy and noisy for my needs — or too quiet?* Is there enough happening locally to keep you interested and prevent you from getting homesick and to ensure that your holidays are more enjoyable?

Remember to find out what the place you are choosing is like at peak season and off season. If everything shuts down at certain times of year you may find it very boring. Alternatively, in peak season the resort may be so packed and busy (and prices in shops and restaurants will reflect this) that you dread going to visit. If you are particularly interested in golf or riding check out the local facilities.

- *What are the medical facilities like?* Even if you are only planning to visit for a few weeks a year you should check these out.

Accidents can happen and you cannot guarantee that you will not fall ill.
- *What are the shopping facilities like?*
- *Is the area desirable?* This will be important when you come to sell or if you want to rent the property out.

Where to look: guidelines

Costa del Sol

Set between Nerja to the east of Malaga and the frontier with Gibraltar, the Costa del Sol is one of the most popular regions. Much of the 160 km of coastline has been heavily developed with high-rise hotels and apartment buildings. It is also one of the most expensive places to buy a property. It also has one of the best climates — not always as hot as the eastern Mediterranean coast in summer but still very mild in winter (often above 60° Fahrenheit in January). It is a part of Andalucia which has very little rain (9–18 inches a year) and some 3000 hours of sunshine a year.

The most well-known towns include Torremolinos, Marbella, Estepona and Fuengirola. But these have become very built up in the last 20 years which may make them less than ideal to live in on a permanent basis. The beaches and bars tend to get overcrowded. However, if you are looking to let out your property you will probably get plenty of interest. For permanent residence you may prefer to look at a small town or resort so that your life is not made a misery by the thousands of tourists descending on the Costa del Sol in the summer.

Malaga, the province's capital, has a busy airport which means that flights are regular and cheap. But Malaga itself is very busy and crowded so a town further away — such as Salobrina or Calahonda — may be more desirable. At the other end of this coast the second airport is Gibraltar.

Other places to consider buying include Valez-Malaga and Nerja, which stands on a cliff at the foot of the towering Sierra del Almijara mountains and is one of the most beautiful towns in Spain, 30 miles from Malaga

Further inland prices are cheaper but your home can still be in easy driving distance of the coast. Mountain villages include Jimena de la Frontera, Casares, Benahavis, Istan, Monda, Ojen and Coin.

Sotogrande is a large resort with golf courses and marina which can be reached from Gibraltar.

The Costa del Sol has some of the best facilities. In addition to golf courses, there are yachting harbours, fishing, bullfights and of course a jet-set nightlife in some resorts such as Marbella.

Prices. You can buy a five-bedroom villa with a separate two-bedroom house to let out or use for guests from £200,000. It would have fetched £300,000 in 1989. A Mijas house with half an acre and granny flat has dropped from £249,000 to £185,000. This gives an indication of the sort of properties you can now snap up at bargain prices. A two-bedroom town house starts from £56,000 and a three-bedroom from £65,000 upwards. A two-bedroom villa ranges from £90,000 to £100,000 and a three-bedroom from £110,000 to £120,000. These prices have increased by about £10,000 in the last two years. Apartments start at around £28,000–£30,000 for a one-bedroom, and £38,000 to £60,000 for a two-bedroom. Price depends on how fashionable the resort is, and how near the property is to the sea.

Typical of the price rises among country homes (which are increasingly in demand) is a three-bedroom detached country house with grounds which was on sale at under £80,000 in 1993, rose to £90,000 by 1996 and is set to fetch at least £120,000 by 1999.

Often homes can be bought ready furnished — which saves on the cost of taking your own with you or spending weeks trying to find the right items and getting them delivered. For example, at the end of 1996 a detached one-bedroom villa, with large terraces, satellite TV, garage and garden could be bought furnished for £44,000.

Costa Blanca

This is the other well-known coast with Alicante, the capital, very popular with tourists. Not only does it have an international airport, but also a harbour, shopping centre, excellent restaurants, museums, sporting facilities and schools.

This has made it popular with Britons who tend to live in nearby towns and resorts rather than in the hustle of the city itself. The other major town on the Costa Blanca is Valencia and the climate is almost as hot as the Costa Brava in summer but has much warmer winters.

The Costa Blanca stretches for some 130 miles from Valencia in the north to Alicante in the south. Just as its name the White Coast implies, the beaches are clean and sandy. But the coast is not the only attraction and inland, away from the beaches and the rocky coast, you will be greeted with scenic views ranging from mountainous backdrops to fertile green valleys of orange, lemon and olive groves. Heading southwards down the map, the main coastal towns popular with British buyers are Denia, Moraira, Calpe and Javea. Styles of property that are available in these areas vary greatly from holiday apartments (two bedrooms from £40,000) to residential bungalows in a complex (two bedrooms from £50,000) to detached villas nestling around the coastline (two bedrooms from £60,000 with an extra £10,000 for a pool).

Further inland, in Orba and in the Jalon valley area (famed for its annual almond blossom and local wines) you will find predominantly detached villas which are marketed at slightly lower prices than those on the coast.

The town of Altea, dominated by its fourteenth-century church, blends well with some of the modern developments that are built into the surrounding hills. Prices in the desirable Altea hills development start from £67,000 for a two-bedroom duplex style apartment with communal pool and for a two-bedroom town house with communal pool, from £77,000.

Benidorm, having shrugged off its lager-lout image, today attracts a more wealthy Spanish crowd, mainly from Madrid, which is only three hours drive away. Although one-bedroom apartments are still affordable, starting at £40,000.

South of the bustling city of Alicante is the town of Santa Pola which is famous for its seafood dishes. Two-bedroom apartments start from £42,500.

The seaside town of Torrevieja which is a short drive from Alicante's airport is surrounded by two large, natural saltwater lagoons. It has a cosmopolitan feel with bars and restaurants, excellent shopping, and one of Spain's largest street markets. There are numerous beaches, golf courses and a marina. This area now offers some of the best value for money for homebuyers on the Costa Blanca with two-bedroom apartments and bungalows from as little as £25,000 and two-bedroom detached villas from an incredible £47,000. It is no wonder that it is increasingly popular among British house-hunters.

The Costa as a whole escaped the blight of over-inflated prices during the 1980s and, as a result, it has retained its credibility as a sound and stable investment.

Costa Brava

This is another popular Spanish coastal region as it is the easiest one to reach by car. Just over the border with France, the Costa Brava is the nearest coast for motorists from Britain. The drawback is that it is not quite as warm as in the south but the average number of hours of sunshine still exceeds 300 in July. While temperatures often exceed 90° Fahrenheit in August, in winter the climate is less mild. It is quite humid with between 20 and 31 inches of rain a year. This rugged coast runs from the frontier town of Le Perthus to Blanes.

It is part of Catalonia and major resorts include Blanes, Lloret de Mar, Tossa de Mar, San Feliu, Palamos, Llafranch, Aiguablava, Estartit, La Escala, Rosas and Port Bou. The major towns are Gerona, an historical town founded at the confluence of the rivers Ter and Onar, and San Feliu de Guixois. The nearest major city and airport is Barcelona. The coastline is not as spoilt as some in the south. To the north of Palamos, there are pleasant small towns and villages in areas such as La Foscal, Sa Riera, Sa Tuna and Aiguablava. Further inland there is the town of Bagur, popular with wealthy Spaniards. And Las Rosas and Cadaques are known for their popularity with painters and writers.

Prices: These are comparable with the north of the Costa Blanca. For a two-bedroom apartment in a modern marine development and close to the large beach in Figueras, you would pay only £40,000 (prices end of 1996). One-bedroom apartments can be snapped up in some fishing ports from £15,000.

Costa Dorada

This is a few miles south from the Costa Brava and also enjoys a hot climate in the summer but again becomes much cooler in winter. It is less accessible than many of the other major tourist regions but can be reached from Barcelona. Its main town is Sitges, one of the prettiest and most elegant resorts in this region.

Costa de la Luz

This is between Cadiz and Huelva on the southern Atlantic coast and translated means the 'coast of light'. It runs up to the Portuguese border and has miles of deserted beaches. The nearest airports are Gibraltar, Jerez de la Frontera and Seville, and the terrain is varied: there are good beaches, some mountainous parts and fertile plains.

This is a less well-known area than the Costa del Sol. As Malaga tends to be one of the most popular airports for British tourists and it is some distance away, the area is more popular with Spaniards than many other coastal areas. Tarifa on the border of the Costa de la Luz is the southernmost town in Spain and is just eight miles from Africa. Cadiz is the major city. There is a massive nature reserve and national park called Doñana by the mouth of the River Guadalquivir.

Inland is the city of Seville, one of the hottest places in Spain with up to 13 hours of sunshine a day and temperatures often exceeding 100° Fahrenheit. With its many cultural attractions this region is ideal if you are looking for more than just sun, sea, sand and sangria. Seville also has an airport but flights tend to be more expensive than to the coastal airports. Other attractions are the sherry towns of Jerez de la Frontera, El Puerto de Santa Maria and Sanlucar de Barrameda. The drawbacks are that the Atlantic can be a rough sea, it can be windy and there are fewer developments and as a result fewer facilities.

Costa Almeria and Costa Calida

These are on the south-east corner of Spain and although on the Mediterranean coast have been less well developed than the rest of the coastline because in the past they have been hard to get to. One of the most well-known resorts in this area is La Manga (although it is not generally residential) — a strip of land with the Mediterranean on one side and the Mar Menor, a shallow inland sea, on the other. There is an international airport at Almeria which is relatively new and this region is likely to be developed further.

The coast of the Murcia province is the Calida. The largest town is Cartagena, which has important military and naval installations and is also a manufacturing and shopping town. The town of Murcia is in the hills 32km from the sea. Almeria is the large commercial town on this coast.

Other places where residential property has been built to cater for the tourist trade include Mojacar, Adra, Almerimar, Aguadulce and Roquetas de Mar.

Further east from La Manga good beaches can be found at Mazarron and Aguillas.

Northern Spain

The Cantabrian coast set on the Bay of Biscay is less well known. The countryside is more lush and mountains project into the sea. Sandy beaches and fishing villages make it very beautiful. The biggest city is Bilbao which can be reached by ferry from Britain. The adjoining province of Guipuscoa adjoins the Cantabrian coast and stretches up to the border with France. Its most important town is San Sebastian.

But it has one drawback — the weather. It often rains one day out of three, and although hot in summer, the winters can be very harsh. Set to the north-west of the mainland the Atlantic coast has hundreds of fishing ports which make it look similar to Cornwall. It is quite mountainous with pine trees making it suitable for those who cannot bear the hot summers of the southern resorts. Coastal property prices are comparable with those in the other costas but it is still possible to snap up very cheap properties inland.

The Balearic Islands

These enjoy a Mediterranean climate but are cooled by sea breezes.

Majorca

This is the largest island in the group (1405 square miles/3640 square kilometres). It is 150km off the Valencia mainland and attracts some three million tourists a year.

Although it has been heavily developed, there are more remote places to live further inland and away from the bay of Palma. The biggest resorts are Magaluf, El Arenal, Illetas, Ca'n Pastilla, Palma Nova and Cala Mayor.

On the east coast most of the development has taken place at Cala Figuera, Cala d'Or, Porto Cristo, Cala Millor and Cala Bona.

To the north-west, the hilly part of the island, Soller and Valldemossa are the bigger towns with the favourite northern residential areas Pollensa, Alcudia and Ca'n Picafort.

Although we think of Majorca as being heavily developed, there are places where you can live in tranquillity particularly in the rugged and mountainous north-west coast of the island which is still relatively undeveloped. And on the east coast, the fertile plains and sandy coves are also quiet with many isolated sandy beaches.

Prices. Small flats in the busy tourist resorts can be bought for £25,000. A restored four-bedroomed farmhouse set in several acres of well-kept land with outbuildings and spectacular views will cost around £250,000.

Minorca

This is the second largest island some 40km from Majorca, and with its own airport. It is just 30 miles wide and 12 miles deep and has a rolling green landscape with golden, sandy beaches. It is less developed as a tourist resort than Majorca. Mahon is the capital city and the other main town is Ciudadela on the west coast which has a picturesque harbour and excellent fish restaurants. The newer resorts are located mainly on the south and east coasts at Santo Tomas, Son Bou, Cal en Porter, Binibeca, Villa-Carlos and El Grao. On the north coast there are settlements at Fornells and Cala Morell. Watch out for cool winds during the winter.

Prices. Detached homes can be bought from between £50,000 and £150,000 and apartments from between £30,000 and £50,000. Most new developments come with fitted kitchens and communal pools but watch out for expensive annual management fees and rates which can add up to £1500 a year.

Ibiza

This is the third largest island (570 sq km) and located 40km west of Majorca. The island averages 300 days of sunshine a year. Ibiza town is the capital. The largest towns, San Antonio Abad and Santa Eulalia del Rio are heavily touristic. More geared to those looking to buy a home are Cala Longa and Roca Lisa.

Prices. An apartment overlooking the front in a large block can be bought from around £35,000 furnished and sleeping up to four.

The Canary Islands

These islands lie off the coast of Morocco in the Atlantic and are only 70 miles from the coast of Africa. Of the seven islands, Gran Canaria, Tenerife, Fuerteventura, Lanzarote and La Palma are the most developed and have enough public services and medical facilities to make them desirable for holiday homes or even permanent residence. They enjoy a climate which is almost like a perpetual UK summer but more humid.

Tenerife

This is the largest of the islands attracting nine million British tourists each year. With £500 million upgrading of the island's facilities scheduled for the next few years, property buyers are at last moving back to the market which went from boom to bust overnight. Building virtually stopped in the slump from August 1989 when prices dropped 30 per cent. Property prices have since stabilised and the market is now strong with demand clearly outstripping supply.

The island has a year-round holiday season. The island splits in two and is dominated by Spain's highest peak, Mount Teide. To the south there are sandy beaches and to the north a dramatic coastline with rich sub-tropical vegetation and exotic flowers. The climate also varies: the north of the island is less sunny as cloud can accumulate over Mount Teide which also creates more humidity. As a result, prices are slightly cheaper in the north unlike the south, which has all year round sunshine and is on the same latitude as Florida but without the same high humidity.

Inland, away from the heavily developed resorts, there is still a natural beauty to the countryside with the scenic Orotava Valley and Las Canadas national park.

Facilities on the island include watersports, a busy nightlife and golf. Quieter resorts include Puerto Santiago, a fishing village with harbourside shops and cafés and Playa Paraiso famous for its lido. El Beril has a small beach and tranquil atmosphere. The most popular resorts are Playa de Las Américas, Puerto de la Cruz, Los Gigantes and Los Cristianos. Those looking for quieter and more sedate areas and retirement homes tend to buy to the north of the island.

The island is also famous for its timeshare developments. Flights take around four hours and can be snapped up very cheaply. Living costs are low.

Prices. Studios in the heavily developed Playa de Las Americas and Los Cristianos start at around £25,000 and one-bedroom apartments from around £32,000. The price of a two-bedroom bungalow in the quieter Puerto de la Cruz begins at around £50,000. Timeshares start at around £2000. Expats looking for a permanent rather than holiday home tend to favour the Orotava Valley.

Gran Canaria is also an island of contrasts and is often referred to as a miniature continent. It has bustling resorts, fishing villages, a thriving city — Las Palmas — sugar canes, banana plantations, papaya and mango trees as well as a mountainous landscape and long stretches of Sahara-like sand dunes. Property prices are 10 to 15 per cent more expensive than in Tenerife due to the German influx which has pushed house prices up.

Lanzarote has a unique character with vineyards, palm trees and traditional whitewashed villages as well as an extraordinary lunar landscape, volcanic hillsides and mysterious rock formations. There are several popular holiday resorts — mostly to the east of the island near the airport. These include Puerto del Carmen, Costa Teguise, Arrecife and Playa de Los Pocillos. Prices in Lanzarote and the other remaining Canary Islands are similar to those in the north of Tenerife.

La Palma is the most westerly of the Canary Islands, 20 minutes' flight from Tenerife. The capital Santa Cruz de La Palma is a lively seafront town with a reasonable selection of shops and restaurants. The interior is beautiful with stunning mountains, sweeping woodlands and a lovely coastline.

La Gomera was unspoilt until a few years ago but is now under extensive construction mainly with large apartment developments aimed at local investors. You get there by ferry from the south coast of Tenerife (the journey takes just over an hour). It is heavily wooded, mountainous, has spectacular valleys and the National Park of Garajonay.

Fuerteventura may be too quiet to consider as a place to buy a home. It has miles of sandy beaches and is favoured as a destination for a relaxing winter break.

What type of property?

This will usually depend on how much you can afford and where you are buying. On the most popular costas you may be restricted to an apartment but further inland a villa may be within your budget. Here are some things to consider about certain types of property before you start looking.

Pueblo-style: These are groups of terraced houses linked by pedestrianised precincts or walkways. Housing is high density and you will share the maintenance costs of communal areas.

Detached villas: These are obviously more expensive and you will have to pay all the bills yourself. However, in exchange for privacy you will have no one on site to look after your home in your absence unless you buy on an estate.

Apartments: You will be subject to the rules of the building and have to share maintenance costs. This is often a cheaper way to buy and you may be able to afford facilities such as swimming pools and tennis courts that you would not be able to buy if you opted for a more expensive house. There is also more likelihood that there will be someone on site to keep an eye on your flat when you are not there. Apartments with a sea view are very desirable and as such are likely to be very expensive.

In Spain properties with communal facilities such as shared gardens and swimming pools are covered by the Law of Horizontal Ownership. This means that it is up to the owners to decide how their development is to be maintained and managed day by day. Thus the community is run according to the decisions approved by the majority of owners. However, the rights of minorities have to be protected as well. Each community of owners has its own regulations known as statutes or 'estatutos' which detail which parts are jointly owned. So before buying a property of this type you should check out your obligations. You will have to pay your share of expenses and will be required to maintain your property, allow work to be carried out if new services are required for other owners (such as work on water pipes and mains drainage) and obey the community rules. A representative known as the Presidente is elected every year and is responsible for ensuring that the community's affairs are run in the interests of everyone and will organise votes by residents to ensure that everyone has a say in matters that affect all occupants.

Failure to pay your community expenses can result in repossession.

Timeshare

Those looking for a holiday home for very little outlay and who do not want the problems associated with leaving a holiday home unoccupied for several months of the year may want to consider timeshare.

Although this method of purchase is cheaper than buying outright you should remember that annual management fees can add up.

Most developers are members of schemes which allow you to swap your weeks with someone else's in another resort. Make sure that the developer is financially sound and that maintenance and cleanliness are up to scratch.

Most timeshares are sold on a freehold basis which means that you can freely sell your timeshare — although you are not guaranteed to get your money back.

The costs make timeshares only marginally cheaper over a ten-year period than renting.

Timeshare salespeople can be very persuasive and you are advised not to sign anything or pay any deposit on your first meeting.

Ask other timeshare owners in the development about the quality of the management firm and check if the development is a member of a timeshare exchange scheme such as Interval International or Resort Condominiums International. These organisations only accept timeshares of a suitably high standard (see Part I for more information on timeshares).

Consumer protection for homebuyers

Since 1968 Spain has had a law relating to off-plan sales whereby the developer is required to have a completion guarantee from a financial or credit institution. If you are buying from plans make sure that the developer is abiding by this law, which was updated in a 1989 decree. It requires developers to include detailed references with regard to their title to the development site and the planning consents within the framework of the preliminary contract. There have been cases where the developer did not fully own the land or had a second mortgage or failed to meet planning requirements. As such, a buyer could be left with a massive bill — or worse be forced out of their home because it was built illegally. You should therefore expect all professional vendors (ie developers) and intermediaries (ie estate agents) to supply you with very detailed information and documentation before you make your final decision.

You or your legal adviser should make enquiries at the relevant land registry and municipal authority to verify that:

- The vendor has registered title to the property (ie they are selling you something they legally own). If the title is unregistered follow the advice of your legal adviser as there is risk associated with purchase from an unregistered owner.
- There are no mortgages or other charges registered on the property. If the property is not 'libra de cargas' (free of charges) it is almost certainly unsafe to buy.
- Planning consents have been obtained and complied with and building regulations have also been complied with. General enquiries as to plans for future adjacent development can be usefully coupled with these enquiries. After all, you may find that your isolated and peaceful new villa is about to become part of a massive complex.
- The vendor is up to date with the payments of acquisition, property, municipal and wealth taxes. You or your legal adviser must also calculate the liability to municipal gains tax 'plus valia', if any, and negotiate which party is to be liable for payment.

Greater consumer protection has also been extended to cover conveyancing lawyers — known as a 'notario' (notary) in Spain. In 1992 a decree increased the obligations of notaries with regard to land registry searches made immediately prior to signing a public deed of purchase and sale.

In effect the notary is under an obligation to make an application by fax to the competent land registry for a title report which has to be dated no more than four working days prior to the date of signing of the public deed. This decree came into force from 6 August 1993. The Land Registry has to fax the report in question direct to the notary. In addition and immediately following completion the notary is able to fax to the registrar details of the deed which has been signed in order that the registrar can make an annotation in his or her diary of documents received, thereby giving provisional protection for that document potentially within minutes of the document having been signed in the notary's office. Notaries can opt out of this provided both parties consent. But as it provides valuable protection, this is not advisable.

If you are conducting your property conveyancing at a Spanish Consulate then you will not be covered by the provision of the new search decree. So it may be advisable to conduct your conveyancing within mainland Spain to reduce the risks and improve your protection.

The conveyancing stage by or to a Spanish resident, including a developer, must take place in Spain. But the resale involving payment outside Spain does not have to take place in Spain.

Legal requirements

In addition to the taxation requirements listed above and the requirement to register for a non-resident taxpayer number, British home-buyers who are non-resident should record their investment in the Foreign Investment Registry. It can be difficult if not impossible to make a sale in the future if your property has not been registered. The form you will need is MC–3A.

The notario also has to ensure that relevant exchange control regulations have been followed and will require certain other documents including a certificate from the bank stating that money has come from outside Spain.

Getting legal advice

The 'abogado' is the name given to a barrister. These are the lawyers who give counselling. The 'notario' only oversees the conveyancing. You will need to use a notary but should also consider getting advice from an independent lawyer. Remember that the lawyer employed by the vendors will not be acting for you and if you involve a notary he will not necessarily be looking out for pitfalls and protecting your interests, only handling the conveyancing.

It is recommended that you do not sign documents until you have taken legal advice and do not use the same lawyer as the vendor. However, only one notary will be involved in the conveyancing document. You can either use a Spanish lawyer or one of the small number of UK lawyers with experience in this field.

If you cannot be there in person you can appoint someone to represent you by a special power of attorney known as the 'escritura de poder de compraventa' granted before a notary public or by the Spanish Consulate in London.

As all stages in the property purchase process will involve understanding or signing documents in Spanish, ask for or obtain written translations before signing any document. Some developers (although not usually individual vendors) like buyers to sign an option or contract of reservation, usually against the payment of a nominal deposit. Think twice before signing. Demand for property is not usually so great that you will lose out if you don't sign immediately. It is not safe to sign a document before making title and planning searches as you could then lose out if you find there is a problem and want to pull out. Check whether the deposit is returnable if you do not proceed.

If you are buying a property which is part of an estate or block of flats you should obtain:

- a copy of the co-ownership rules;
- a copy of the latest accounts of the community of owners; and
- a statement from the managers of the vendor's balance of account with the community.

When it comes to the exchange of contracts you will be required to sign a 'Contrato Privado' (Private Contract). You need not use a notary at this stage, but remember that the Private Contract is a legally binding commitment to buy on the terms stated in the document. Private Contracts are not lengthy documents but will contain the names and description of the parties, a description of the property, the price, the method of payment and any general or special conditions negotiated by the parties as well as the statutory matters imposed by the 1989 Decree (see above). Not less than 10 per cent of the purchase price will be payable on signing the Private Contract and a higher figure is frequently sought by developers. Where stage payments are to be made before Legal Title is given, particularly in the case of developments in the course of construction, make rigorous enquiries to satisfy yourself that the vendor is solvent and that his building programme is adequately funded or bonded (see consumer protection section).

You should also check whether contents and/or the cost of connecting water, gas and electricity (if not already supplied) are included in the price.

Although these private contracts are legally binding, they do not prevent creditors making a prior claim on the property or the seller selling to another buyer or mortgaging the property.

The next stage is completion. This will be on a date stipulated in the Private Contract or, if it is a new development, could be upon completion of construction. You are at risk until a formal document, 'escritura publica de compraventa' (known usually as escritura), transfers the ownership to you. It has to be prepared and witnessed, a function undertaken by a notary and then registered in the Land Registry. Because you are still at risk it is essential that you do not delay at this stage. Another search should be made when the property is registered.

A non-resident purchaser must prove that he or she is a non-resident by producing a certificate issued by the local Spanish police station, or if there is insufficient time to obtain it prior to signing, produce the same subsequently and prior to registration in the Land Registry.

You will then receive the 'escritura', a certified copy of which, known as the 'primera copia' (first copy) will be your title deed. This is a more detailed document than the Private Contract and will state the names and descriptions of the parties, a full description of the property referring to rights of way and use, boundaries, unit location within a development (if applicable), size and make-up of unit, the title of the vendor (with Land Registry references), the price, method of payment or receipt of the price, as the case may be, and any special conditions.

In addition the document should also contain a statement or warranty that:

- the vendor is the legal owner of the property;
- the property is sold with vacant possession; and
- that the property is not subject to any charges. (See the consumer protection section for the details of the requirements of notaries to conduct searches.) If the property is subject to charges full details of those recorded against the property should be listed.

Warning: Unlike English law, debt can attach to property so if you are buying from a seller in arrears his creditors could take possession. That is why it is essential that the notary public checks with the Land Registry a second time.

Buyers are required to have their first copy registered at the relevant Registry. Remember to ask the notary to do this for you as he or she will be able to gain priority for the Deed by sending a fax to the Land Registry stating that a Deed has been signed concerning a specified property. The time taken to complete registration can be up to a year so don't forget to chase this up.

Get the 'escritura' translated and properly checked. The Registry then converts the 'escritura de compraventa' into an 'escritura publica' or title deed.

Surveys

Structural surveys are not common but that does not mean that you shouldn't get one done. It could save you a lot of money in the long run if there is a major fault with the property. The consumer protection laws covering developers means that they must give details of construction and insulating materials used, fire safety measures, the general plans of the property and a plan of the public utility services along with copies of licences and building permissions. Some may want to dispense with a detailed survey on a new property.

If you are planning to buy an older property make sure the sewage arrangements are adequate as some still have cesspits.

Illegal buildings

There have been horror stories in newspapers about Brits who bought homes in Spain only to find that they were in breach of planning permission and were then demolished.

This should not happen if you follow the correct procedures. However, you should be aware of the law of the coastal areas — the Ley de Costas — approved in 1988 to protect the coastline from being ruined by even more development. No new construction is allowed on designated beaches and coasts and the height of some buildings further inland is also restricted as is the proximity of buildings. Existing properties are not affected provided they have the required building licences, planning permission and clear titles. However, if you buy a home in one of the designated areas remember that you will probably not be allowed to extend or enlarge your property.

> **John Howell & Co**
> Solicitors & International Lawyers
> _The_ specialists In Spain
> **Why us?**
> • We have 10 years experience • We do only work related to Spain
> • We have our own Spanish lawyers • All of our lawyers are bilingual
> • You have the security of dealing with fully insured,
> specialist English solicitors
> 17 Maiden Lane, Covent Garden, London WC2E 7NA
> Telephone 0171 420 0400   Fax 0171 836 3626

Your lawyer should check at the town hall, 'Ayuntamiento', that the developer of a new property has proper planning permission. The 'Registro de la Propiedad' can provide a 'Nota Simple' for the property including details of any mortgage outstanding.

How much will buying cost?

Be prepared for a much larger bill than at home. You will have to pay Value Added Tax — known as IVA or 'impuesto sobre el valor anadido' in Spain — on new properties of 7 per cent to the developer and 0.5 per cent to the local tax office. IVA is also paid on the land at 16 per cent. In the Canary Islands, the purchase tax (IGTE) is 4.5 per cent and is payable instead of IVA. A further 0.5 per cent is payable in both cases to the local tax office.

For the resale of properties the tax is also high but in this case the 6 per cent is payable to the local tax office. This tax, which is similar to stamp duty, is often collected by the notary as your agent. But again, make sure this has been paid. Don't be tempted to try and cut your tax bill by underdeclaring the price in the 'escritura' as this is a tax fraud and can result in a large fine. You could also be losing out if you claim the property costs less on purchase, as when you come to sell you will end up with a larger capital gains tax liability. This tax on private sales is known as the 'impuesto sobre transmisiones' (ITP).

You will also have to pay notarial fees, Land Registry fees, other legal costs if you seek independent legal advice, the cost of translating legal documents and you will also have to pay for the notary or lawyer to complete Form MC-3A (see section on taxes) even if you have not brought money into Spain.

And don't forget removal costs, the costs of flying out to Spain (if you do not already live there) and survey costs if you decide to have a survey.

In all, the costs will add around 10 per cent to the cost of the purchase of your property. But allow for a little more just in case there are any last minute problems.

Notario charges are calculated according to the declared value of the property and the purchaser is usually liable to pay all of them.

In addition in urban areas there is another tax known as the 'plus valia' which is charged once per ownership on the capital gain during the ownership of the property. The seller should be liable for this tax.

Lawyers' fees are about 4 per cent of the purchase price.

What costs will I have to meet after purchase?

As many overseas buyers purchase flats or houses on estates which provide extra facilities such as swimming pools or a caretaker, you will have to pay towards the running of these as you would at home with the service charge on a flat. If you are buying an individual property, you must be prepared to pay for maintenance and repairs. And don't forget the obvious costs including gas, water, electricity and telephone charges as well as insurance premiums. If you are buying a new property or are planning to renovate an old one you may have to pay to connect these services.

Then there are municipal taxes (like rates or the council tax) which are charged at 0.4–1.17 per cent in urban areas and 0.3–1.11 per cent in rural areas; income tax (whether or not you let your property) charged at 25 per cent to non-residents; and wealth tax (0.2–2.5 per cent). For more information see the section on taxes.

And don't forget the cost of a tax representative resident in Spain to be responsible for income and wealth tax, as you have to appoint one by law or face a fine.

Payment of these bills will be easier if you open a local bank account.

Bank accounts

It is essential to open a bank account in Spain if you want to pay bills, transfer money and receive income for things like holiday lets. The types of account include a resident's peseta account and a non-resident's peseta account. Alternatively, if you do not want or do not need to convert all your money into pesetas you can set up a foreign currency deposit or current account.

When writing out Spanish cheques remember that dates must be in words and that in Spain full stops are used instead of the comma and sums must be written out in full in Spanish. To cross a cheque write 'y Cia'.

It will probably be best for you to keep your existing credit card rather than take out a Spanish one.

Raising the finance

If you are buying from a developer you may not have to pay the whole purchase price immediately and may be offered up to five years to settle the full amount.

If the seller demands payment in full a Spanish bank will lend up to 75 per cent although in practice it may only be possible to borrow half the value of the property. Mortgages tend to be for shorter periods than in the UK, usually up to a maximum of ten years. However, in practice it may be easier to get a loan from a British bank or a lender prepared to lend on overseas property, but you may have to secure the loan on your UK home.

Get your mortgage in sterling if you have a sterling income to avoid exchange fluctuations affecting your ability to pay.

What if I want to sell?

You may love living in Spain so much that you want to buy a bigger, better property. Or maybe you want to move to a different area or even back home. If so, make sure the local agent you use is properly licensed. Don't forget that if you are a non-resident of Spain, the buyer must withhold 10 per cent of the price of the property and pay it to the district tax office to cover capital gains tax (see section on taxes).

You will also have to provide form MC-3A if you are a non-resident, as evidence that you bought the property in accordance with foreign investment rules. The buyer will pay for most of the incidental costs but as the vendor you will be liable for the 'plus valia' or added taxes unless otherwise agreed under the terms of the Private Contract.

Taxes

Spain has substantially tightened its tax net in recent years to increase central and local government revenues. The Spanish government was well aware that it was not receiving the revenues it should have been from income tax on rental income and capital gains tax on resales between non-residents.

It has therefore become necessary to obtain a fiscal identity number immediately upon acquiring an asset in Spain (for non-Spaniards this is an NIE) and existing owners are required to do the same. Anyone who resides in Spain for more than 183 days a year is liable to pay Spanish income tax even if they are not permanent residents. Failure to apply voluntarily for a fiscal number can effectively prevent you from conducting your financial affairs.

Under the 1994 regulations, non-resident property owners have the option, provided they own only one dwelling, of notifying the address of that dwelling as an address for official tax notifications from the Spanish Revenue or they must appoint a tax representative who must be responsible for filing the declarations. You can do this yourself, but it may be better to invest in a tax representative. Although it will cost you, you could end up saving far more in the long run. Using the simplified option there is a risk of communications not being attended to at the proper time and the consequent risk of tax enforcement against the property itself, potentially again without the knowledge of the property owner.

Non-residents of Spain who own only one Spanish dwelling no longer need to have a fiscal representative who is living in Spain. However, as they require a fiscal identification number and have to submit an income tax return each year this may be advisable.

You will not get UK mortgage tax relief on mortgages to buy a Spanish property. If you rent out your Spanish property, you should discuss with an accountant: the tax liabilities in Spain and the UK, what relief you can claim for interest on buying the property and how you can offset any Spanish taxes paid on the rental income against your UK tax liability. The difficulties in dealing with this may make it easier to borrow from a UK bank.

Capital gains tax

Capital gains tax collection from non-residents has also been changed in recent years: the purchaser from a non-resident must now withhold 10 per cent of the gross amount and deposit this with the relevant local tax office within 30 days of the date of the notarial deed of sale. This means that as a non-resident you will not get your full purchase price when you sell and if you are buying from a non-resident you must remember to follow the procedure. Failure to do so results in the purchaser becoming liable for the vendor's capital gains tax up to 10 per cent which should have been retained.

You should get form 211 if you are paying over the 10 per cent to cover the vendor's capital gains tax liability to the district tax office of the property. The non-resident vendor must then file a detailed capital gains tax return and either pay any additional tax or claim a refund of any overpayment. The form for this is 210.

The system has experienced teething troubles. Files may be handled slowly by the Spanish Revenue and revenue offices are taking a tough line with documentary authority to deal with the file. They are also closely examining receipts for associated transaction costs which are used to reduce the amount of the gross gain. As a result it can be difficult dealing with such matters personally and a professional representation at the time of sale is recommended — if only to deal with the capital gains tax implications. The tax is 20 per cent of the profit — the difference between the original price and the new figure. But this is reduced the longer you hold your property. Relief is 11 per cent of the net gain which is knocked off the tax each and every year after the second year of ownership onwards. After ten years the property is tax free but that is not true in relation to any improvements. This law has just changed and is currently under challenge. Should the challenge be successful then the old tax rate of 35 per cent and the old relief of 5.26 per cent may return.

Residents who sell their home at a profit are allowed to reinvest the proceeds in another property without paying tax. Any excess which is not reinvested is added to income for the year and taxed at the appropriate rate.

Plus valia

In addition there is the 'plus valia' tax — the increase in the value of the land since the last sale. It is based on the official value, 'castral', not market value and the rate varies depending on location and length of time between sales of the plot.

But many vendors will find these taxes are low or non-existent because any increases in land value or property prices have been low. It is charged whether or not you are a resident, and is a municipal tax which can be charged every ten years. Make sure you do not inherit a massive tax liability when you buy a property.

Property tax

The new 'impuesto especial' is a 3 per cent tax on official value charged to non-resident companies owning a property in Spain. This tax was introduced to clamp down on tax avoidance.

Tax on rental income

There is also a tax on rental income. Since 1992 Spanish legislation charges a rental income tax against property owners who are non-residents even if they claim not to be letting their property.

The tax is based on the estimated rental value for the period of their occupation per year. It amounts to 0.5 per cent of the official valuation (calculated as 25 per cent of 2 per cent of the 'valor catastral' [1.5 per cent in some cases]).

Wealth tax

Spain also has a wealth tax (an extraordinary tax on assets) which is payable annually. Residents pay this on their worldwide assets, namely everything owned, but are granted a tax-free allowance of 17 million pesetas each (34 million for a couple). Non-residents pay it on all their assets in Spain. However, the rate of tax is very low, only 0.2 per cent on the first 50 million pesetas, which rises to 2.5 per cent at the top end.

Taxes on your home

Don't forget to allow for the annual property tax, the 'impuesto sobre bienes inmuebles' which is based on the official valuation or 'valor catastral' of the property. This varies according to the location and size of the home and the amount paid can be deducted from income tax due.

Then there are rates payable to the local authority. These have been modest in the past but are being increased quite considerably. A rate demand may not be issued so it may be necessary to check the figure due annually at the town hall. If you do not pay up by the set settlement date you may be charged a 20 per cent surcharge. Rates tend to be modest for refuse collection and sewage disposal. These local authority taxes are known as 'tasas'.

Inheritance and succession tax

The 'impuesto sobre sucesiones y donaciones' is charged to non-residents on any asset in Spain. The double tax treaty with Spain should mean that you do not get taxed in both countries but save grief over which country should claim tax by arranging it in advance. Unlike in the UK, inheritance tax in Spain must be paid on transfers between spouses and the inherited property cannot be sold before the dues have been paid.

The tax depends on the value of the assets inherited, the relationship between the deceased and inheritor and the existing wealth of the inheritor at the time they inherit.

Direct descendants get an allowance of 2,470,000 pesetas with an additional 617,000 pts for each child under 21 up to a set maximum. Above this level rates rise from 7.65 per cent on the first 1,235,000 pts to 34 per cent on sums over 123,424,000 pts.

VAT

Finally, don't forget Value Added Tax. VAT is known as IVA in Spain, and is charged at various rates depending on the item being purchased. It is charged on the sale of new homes. If you are setting up permanent residence in Spain you are usually allowed to import your furniture and belongings free of IVA (check with your removal firm).

Tax avoidance

Buying your overseas home through an offshore or tax-shelter company is not the tax break it once was. In effect these companies are now being charged an annual tax of 5 per cent of the catastral value of the property.

But buying your property through an offshore structure can still have advantages when it comes to capital gains tax, transfer tax (ITP) and inheritance tax, but do take good advice as there are various other fiscal considerations to take into account.

Exchange control

There are no restrictions on purchase imposed by either UK or Spanish regulations. No customs duty or VAT is imposed on household goods and clothing imported for personal use by EC citizens. If you are taking up residence in Spain you may also be able to bring in your car free of import duty and VAT (IVA).

Looking after your home

If you are non-resident you should seriously consider getting someone who lives permanently in Spain to look after the property and your affairs. Dealing with wealth tax and income tax returns can be a problem if you only visit a few times a year, so you should appoint a fiscal representative. You will also need someone to ensure that electricity and water bills are paid promptly or else the supply may be cut off.

Letting out your home

As with letting a property at home you should take the usual precautions. Get a deposit to cover damages, ask for the rent in advance and if you are letting the property to people you do not know get a tenancy agreement. This should cover the period of letting, rent, deposit held, extra charges for electricity, etc and responsibility to look after the property.

You will have to add IVA to the rent and pay it to the Finance Ministry and if you let the property you then have to make a tax payment of either 25 per cent of your holiday rental income (or on businesses or profits a rate of 35 per cent of it if you are regarded as an entrepreneur in Spain).

Residence and work permits

No visas are required for those visiting Spain as tourists for up to 90 days. You are allowed a 90-day extension known as a 'permanencia' which can be obtained at a police station. Some evidence of the applicant's ability to finance the continued stay in Spain is required.

If you are planning to remain in Spain for any length of time you will need a residence permit which you can obtain immediately on arrival.

If you are planning to retire in Spain and are an EU national you can obtain your residence permit from the local 'comisaria' or police station by showing your passport and giving proof of sufficient income on which to live, proof of medical insurance from the British social security system or private medical insurance and four passport size photographs. Present your completed application form and fee in the form of a Spanish State Paper which is obtainable from official tobacco shops.

Residence permits for EU nationals are now for five years. See the section on taxation for the tax identification number you will be required to have.

If you have a held a residence permit for four years you will be able to vote in municipal elections. Once you have lived in Spain for ten years you can elect to take Spanish nationality.

Working in Spain

If you are planning to work in Spain and are an EU citizen you will need an EU registration card, issued for one year initially. This can be renewed for a period of five years. The advent of the Single European Market means that EU citizens now have the same opportunity of employment in Spain under similar conditions as a Spaniard. If you find work in Spain your spouse and any dependent children under the age of 21 have full rights to live and work in Spain. Your children will also have the same rights as Spaniards to trade-school education and apprenticeship schemes run by the state. Employment rights extend to unemployment benefit if you lose your job through no fault of your own. But in return for these benefits you must be registered by your employers with the Spanish social security system and have the appropriate contributions and income tax deducted from pay. Check that your employer makes the contributions on your behalf. Increasingly the qualifications of foreign nationals are being recognised in Spain.

Retiring to Spain

Many of the 250,000 Brits living in Spain have gone there to retire, and there are many clubs and societies to cater for their needs.

Retired people can also get a special rate on services including travel, air fares and free entry to museums and libraries which come under the Ministry of Culture.

If your social security contributions are up to date in the UK your rights to medical care are fully transferable to Spain. Obtain the correct form from the UK before you leave and also contact the Overseas Benefits Directorate of the Department of Social Security at Longbenton, Newcastle upon Tyne, NE98 1YX for further details. Retired persons usually fill in form E121. Apply at least a month before leaving the UK.

Anyone retiring to Spain should pay particular attention to their finances. Exchange fluctuations can eat into the amount of income you receive leaving you without enough to live on and remember, Spanish inflation will also reduce your spending power.

You can continue to claim your British pension and it is no longer frozen at the rate payable when you emigrate as it was a decade ago.

Moving home

Importing furniture is almost as straightforward as moving home in the UK. For information contact the British Association of Removers, 3, Churchill Court, 58 Station Road, North Harrow, London HA2 7SA.

The forms you will need are the 'solicitud de franquicia' showing the address of the destination or the form 'vivienda secundaria' if it is a secondary residence. You will also need an inventory showing the value of goods in pesetas, photocopies of the first five pages of your passport (last two pages if you have a new EU passport), proof of application for a residence card or proof of having been a resident of another country for at least the last 12 months.

Finally, don't forget insurance cover.

Language

It is always useful to learn at least a few essential words of Spanish particularly if you are not living in the heart of a major tourist resort. Spanish is a collection of languages. Castilian is spoken by about three-quarters of the population. Catalan is spoken in the north east, Basque in its region and Galician in the north west.

Education

If you are planning to move to Spain and have school age children you will find that there are reasonably good international schools. Details are available from the European Council of International Schools, 21 Lavant Street, Petersfield, Hampshire, GU32 3EL (01730 268 244). Younger children can be started in the Spanish education system which is free and this will help them to integrate into the local community more easily.

However, if you intend to send your child to a British senior school or university it may be better to send them to a private school in Spain. There is a wide choice of British private schools in Spain though not many boarding schools. There is a National Association of British Schools based in Madrid which arranges for schools to be visited regularly by British inspectors. Some teach only British pupils; others have mixed Spanish and British classes.

Health

As an EU citizen you will be entitled to use the Spanish National Health Service but private health insurance may be worthwhile. This will cover such things as post-operative or geriatric care which are not covered by the state scheme. If you only visit your property for holidays your travel insurance should cover health care. Anyone in receipt of a British state pension can join the Spanish National Health Service without paying contributions.

If you are under pensionable age you will have to pay a monthly contribution. Take your passport to the local social security office, the 'Instituto Nacional de Prevision', and they will deal with the necessary documentation and advise you what you will have to pay. If you are working in Spain you will have to join — for others it is voluntary.

Family law

Births and deaths

All births in Spain must be registered at the Civil Registry within eight days. British nationals should register at the British Consulate. Deaths must also be registered at the Registry which is usually at the town hall. Repatriation can cost as much as 100,000–200,000 pesetas.

Wills

Making a will if you own a property abroad is highly advisable. However, provided you have not taken out Spanish nationality or are not legally domiciled in Spain you can be governed by British law. Take out a will in Britain to save confusion.

In Britain you can leave your children out of your will if you do not get along with them, but in Spain there is the law of obligatory heirs, 'herederos forzosos'. If you die leaving children (or if they are no longer alive, grandchildren or great-grandchildren), your estate is divided into three equal parts. A surviving spouse has a life interest in one-third, another third goes to your children (or their offspring if they are no longer alive) and the final third you can do with as you wish. Your estate excludes half the assets acquired during marriage which go to your spouse along with any personal gifts.

Dealing with officials

You will find that everything takes far longer in Spain than in the UK. If you have a complaint concerning officialdom Spain has an ombudsman who deals with these even if you are a foreigner.

Consumer rights

There are new rules in Spain to protect you from cowboy repairmen. These cover most household goods, from washing machines to video recorders. A three-month guarantee is given. You should also be given estimates on any repair and a date by which it should be finished. This estimate is valid for 30 days.

Driving in Spain

You may drive on Spanish roads if you have a current valid driving licence which you must carry with you when driving. As a tourist you must either have a current international driving licence or a British driving licence with an official Spanish translation (the new pink ones have this). However, a resident (ie someone who has lived in Spain for more than one year) in Spain must have a Spanish driving licence. These can be obtained by using the services of a 'gestor' and without taking a new test.

If you are planning to buy a car in Spain — *buyer beware!* Any Spanish car must have two documents: a 'Permiso de Circulacion' which makes it legal to drive and a 'Tarjeta de Inspeccion Tecnica de Vehiculos' which is a certificate of roadworthiness. If you buy or sell a car the transfer document on the back of the Permiso de Circulacion must be completed. The Jefatura Provincial de Trafico should also be notified of the change of ownership. The local car tax is known as the 'impuesto sobre la circulacion de vehiculos'. And the car's identity document is called the 'cedula de identificacion fiscal'.

Cars drive on the right-hand side of the road and drivers must give way to traffic from the right. Wearing seat-belts is compulsory and cars must carry a red warning triangle and display this in the event of a breakdown.

You can import your car without paying duty provided you have owned it for at least six months. But the difference between British and Spanish VAT will be charged. An application for an import licence should be made to the Spanish Customs office in Madrid. Import duty may be charged but will be returned when you obtain a Spanish resident permit. Enquire at the Spanish Consulate for more information.

If you are taking your car to Spain for a holiday get a Green Card from your British insurance company. All Spanish cars must be insured against third-party claims with a Spanish insurance company. This compulsory insurance is called the 'seguro obligatorio'. Extra insurance, which is advisable, is called 'seguro voluntario'.

Telephones

If you want a phone installed you may have to wait. Spain's equivalent of BT is Telefonica. You can pay bills at their offices or by standing order. Bills include the following terms: 'Facturacion' — the period of billing; 'Total a Pajon' — the total amount to pay; 'Cuesto de Abono' — the standing charge; 'Servicio Lectua' — the number of units or 'pasos' you have used; and 'Base Imponible' — the preliminary total before VAT. Bills must be paid within 20 days.

Utilities

The electricity supply in Spain is 220 or 225 volts AC. In parts of the Balearic Islands it may be 110 volts.

Electricity and water bills must be paid promptly or supplies may be cut off, with a subsequent hefty reconnection charge.

There is a standing charge for electricity, payable every two months even if no electricity is used. Bottled gas is cheap and there are no gas mains other than in the larger cities.

Water supply can be erratic and prices are rising. Reserve tanks are ideal to cover periods when the water is turned off.

It is advisable to pay by standing order for all these utilities.

Buying a home in France

Location is one of the most important factors in a property purchase. And France certainly has that in its favour. It is just a few hours from Britain (22 miles across the Channel), making it easy to visit if you choose it as your permanent base or regular holiday haunt. It is also one of the most popular foreign destination for Britons, with almost eight million of us visiting every year.

This fondness for France and its culture, food and pace of life is reflected in the number of us who aspire to own a home there.

Language is another factor in its favour — not only is it the most popular second language taught in Britain (so most of us at least know a few words of classroom French) but English is also their second language, making communication less of a problem than in many other European countries.

And then, of course, there is price. The difference between prices here and there makes France a very tempting location to buy a property. The prospect of buying an unmodernised old farmhouse for just £15,000 has lured many Brits to buy up and then do up homes in France. However, the most desirable areas on the south coast are among the most expensive places to live in Europe.

Lifestyle is the other major attraction — good food, great wine, the relaxed pace of life and a more favourable climate conjure up a café society, sipping pastis in the village square, watching the old men of the village playing boules and soaking up the sun by the Mediterranean as the yachts sail past. It is no wonder that Peter Mayle's *A Year in Provence* caught the British imagination and became a bestseller. We tend to have a very idealistic view of life in France.

Most of us are familiar with France as we probably have visited at least once — even if only on a day trip by ferry. But we don't really know the true France. It is an advanced industrial country in parts — not the rural farming nation that we like to think it is.

France is a far larger country than Britain — double the size — which means that many of the cheaper homes are very remote. France is not as densely populated as Britain with a slightly smaller population of 56 million living in a country of 210,000 square miles. That is why some rural areas have very low property prices. The French themselves do not want to live in a far-flung village with no shops, no jobs and no transport. Homes in the more desirable areas — such as the Riviera — where the French themselves want to buy holiday homes are much more expensive.

The sheer size of France also means that you must not look at it as one country but a series of very different regions where the type and the cost of property varies widely and where customs and traditions and even language often bear no relation to other regions.

There are 95 mainland 'départements' similar to our counties and these in turn make up its 22 regions. In addition France is divided into 20 or so historical provinces — these are the ones we are more familiar with as tourists and include Normandy, Brittany, Provence and Gascony.

France may only be 22 miles away across the Channel but in many respects it is a world apart. So before getting carried away at the prospect of buying far more for your money in France, remember the extra costs — add at least 10 per cent to the purchase price, the extra hassle and the often poor resale market which can mean that homes in France are not a good investment.

In addition, the cost of living in France — particularly in tourist areas — is not always as cheap as it may seem. So you may have to allow for a much larger income than you may have previously thought. Generally, you will need a minimum income of £12,000 (excluding mortgages and/or rents) to live full-time in France but this will not allow you to live the good life.

Where to live in France

The sheer size of France means that you can choose almost any type of location to suit your needs — from the mountains to the coast, from a large bustling market town to a remote farm. Remember to think of France as a series of very different regions rather than look at the country as a whole.

To save on time and money driving hundreds of miles round different regions, first make a list of what you are looking for and what you want out of your life in France.

The following points will help you make up your mind.

Journey time

Are you going to live there permanently or just visit at weekends? The opening of the Channel Tunnel makes properties within a short drive of Paris ideal. Properties within an hour's drive of Calais are particularly popular and still cheap. A farmhouse for £30,000 is quite possible.

Anywhere that is easy to get to from Nice is already very expensive as the flight service is fast (1 hour and 50 minutes from Heathrow or Gatwick with several flights a day) and the airport takes you right into the heart of the most fashionable coastal region. Another region which is easy to get to by plane is Gascony (Toulouse airport is 1 hour and 40 minutes from Gatwick).

Other airports you can fly to direct from Britain are Bordeaux, Lyon, Marseille, Montpellier, Nantes, Perpignan, Strasbourg, Grenoble and, of course, Paris.

Biarritz (Bayonne-Anglet), Fréjus (St Raphael), Hyères (Hyères-Toulon) and Lyon (Satolas) all have airports which you can fly to on internal flights as well as Pontoise, Rouen, Dinard, Cherbourg, Brest, Caen, Le Havre, Quimper and Lourdes. You may find that you can fly to these direct on smaller airlines or special charter flights.

If you are choosing a French airline, Air France has the best service on offer. For internal flights to a larger range of airports Air Inter serves 39 airports from Paris. If you are travelling regularly within France you can buy a season ticket to get up to a 30 per cent reduction. The internal air market has greatly opened up. Fly-drive arrangements are another possibility.

Alternatively, British Airways has regular flights to several airports within France as does British Midland. During the summer months charter flights rather than scheduled flights can be a cheaper alternative.

The French road and motorway system is excellent, and makes most of the country easily accessible. Remember that on autoroutes you will have to pay a toll. In addition there are the Routes Nationales which are trunk roads going through towns. These are not toll roads.

If you are driving on autoroutes to the south of France you may not find it particularly cheap: tolls can add up to £100 or more to the cost of your journey and you will also have to pay for accommodation. However, the French have very cheap motels such as the Formule 1 which cost around £20 per night for a family of three.

Although you may not consider taking the train at home, in France where the country is far larger and therefore journey times by car are longer, consider the train system (SNCF). Services are efficient and fast and you can take take your car on the Motorail to save yourself the exhausting journey of driving for a whole day — or more. Check in advance for discounts and offers for in-week travel and group bookings.

Climate

When you are planning to visit, remember a holiday resort that is a perfect location in the spring and summer may be very miserable in the winter. So don't forget to bear in mind that you may be stuck with a property that you do not want to visit for many months of the year. Imagine what your remote cottage will be like when it is freezing cold in winter; shops and restaurants catering for the summer tourist trade are closed and the weather is too miserable for you to enjoy the outdoor life you have been dreaming of.

View your property at different times of the year to make absolutely sure that you are making the right decision. One of the best ways is to rent in the area first before buying unless you are very familiar with the place.

The absent property owner

Another factor to bear in mind if you are not planning to live in your home permanently is what will happen when you are away. It may be better to pick a property in a complex or in the heart of a town or village where there is someone (or you can appoint someone) to look after your home when it is unoccupied.

If you are looking to get away from it all, picking a remote area where hardly any other non-French live may seem ideal. But ask yourself this: *Why* don't they live there? There may be very good reasons — poor communications and transport and very few facilities. The French themselves may have no option to live there but you have a choice. Don't waste your money and time on making the wrong one.

And remember, if you are looking for a summer holiday home, pick somewhere that the French go for their holidays. In August almost all of France shuts down for annual holidays. If you pick the wrong place your entire village, bar one shop, could close as the rest of the population goes 'en vacance'.

Where to look: guidelines

Note: Prices in this section are based on those at the end of 1996 and at an exchange rate of just over 8 francs to the pound.

The south of France

Half of all foreigners living in France live in the south of France between Lyon and the coast. This takes in the Midi, Provence, the Côte d'Azur with its fashionable resorts including Nice, Cannes and St Tropez.

The coast itself stretches from the border with Spain to Monaco with most popular areas between Marseille and Menton and the 'départements' of the Var and the Alpes-Maritimes. Properties more than 20 miles away from the coast and the most fashionable resort towns and villages tend to be cheaper but they are still expensive in comparison to other places in France.

The climate is the obvious attraction, along with the fact that there is a thriving social life, with many bars, restaurants, golf courses and beaches. And of course a large British community. Many of those buying in the south of France already know other people who have homes there too.

For most it is the Riviera or nothing — otherwise what is the point of buying in France? And to many French, anything west of Cannes is considered to be almost Spain and not the south of France. As a result property prices to the west are far cheaper.

The coast splits like this: the Languedoc-Roussillon region starts at the eastern border with Spain and stretches towards Marseille. This region is the least fashionable and therefore the cheapest. Then from Marseille to St Tropez is Provence and the Côte d'Azur which includes Fréjus, Cannes, Nice and Antibes. From St Tropez east towards the Italian border and Monaco is by far the most desirable and most expensive stretch of coastline.

But even along the south coast the climate can be poor. In the Languedoc-Roussillon region there are the winds and Provence is plagued by the *mistral* — the fierce wind that blows up from North Africa especially in the spring and autumn — and the Côte d'Azur can also suffer forest fires as well as violent thunderstorms. What makes this coastline so popular is the climate which is far more clement than that on the Atlantic coast.

The Alpes-Maritimes and Monte Carlo (although not in France as it is part of Monaco on the border with Italy) along with Cannes, Nice, Villefranche and Beaulieu are among the most desirable, and expensive, places to live, along with properties in Cap Ferrat and the hills around these towns. Cogolin, Port Grimaud, Ramatuelle and Cavalaire are the most expensive in Var. For those looking for prize properties away from the coast the most expensive areas are around Grasse, St Paul, Vence and Valbonne. You will get little change from £250,000 for a villa round there, but lettings are relatively good so you could recoup some of the outlay.

If you are looking in this region it is likely to be price not location that dictates your choice as you will probably not be able to afford the location you really desire.

Facilities are excellent, ranging from restaurants to golf courses and marinas to beaches. For skiers, living closer to the Alps means that you can have a holiday home that you can use in both summer and winter. For instance, you can easily drive within a few hours from the Hautes d'Alpes de Provence where you can ski to the Alpes-Maritimes where the beaches can be found.

On the other side of France you can commute from the Pyrénées-Orientales to the Roussillon and Perpignan beaches. And of course, do not forget Andorra, which although it is not part of France, is accessible from Perpignan and that coast.

Roads along the south coast make it easy to travel around — apart from August when the whole of France, Britain, Germany and Italy seems to be on the road.

The main road south is the Autoroute du Sud which forks left into the Autoroute du Soleil (road of the sun) and turns into La Provençale. It forks right into the Languedossiene which in turn ends up up being La Catalane which passes along the Languedoc-Roussillon coast.

Prices. It is difficult to generalise as in the most fashionable areas some properties can only be afforded by millionaires. You will be lucky to get an apartment near to the beach in a fashionable seaside resort for less than £100,000 or a villa for the same price further inland.

However, in Languedoc, town houses packed cosily together in little streets or villages can be bought for £30,000 plus, 20 minutes' drive inland from the sea according to property agents A House in France.

The Biarritz, St Jean de Luz, Hendaye area is expensive, as is anywhere near a golf course — and this part of France has the best. The adjoining Pau region is also not cheap and both areas have very few cottages; even among the villas there are very few resales.

In French Catalonia, the region around Perpignan close to Spain, you can get a small two-bedroom terraced house in good condition from around £28,000. The large 'Mas', farmhouses peculiar to this area and Provence, can start from £100,000 in good condition. 'Mas' with land and stables and even vineyards start from £150,000 and run to £650,000.

Provence is not as expensive as people believe. However, around Aix-en-Provence is the 'arm-and-a-leg' category. Elsewhere properties start at £50,000 and larger villas from £125,000. But for a decent farm with outhouses and some land in Aix-en-Provence you will be looking at paying at least £215,000.

The Riviera breaks into Var and the Alpes-Maritimes, the latter being the more expensive. You can get a nice villa in the hills behind Hyères from £100,000 in Var whereas in the Côte d'Azur from Cannes to Menton you would probably only get a one-bedroom flat for that price.

Inland areas around St-Paul-de-Vence and Seillans are also expensive. For those looking for something cheaper, terraced village houses in the hills are less expensive, but not as cheap as those nearer the Pyrénées. The drawback is that these do not have garages or gardens and the narrow cobbled streets mean they may not get much sunshine either.

The Alps

This breaks down into the Alpes de Haute-Provence, the Hautes-Alpes, the Savoie and Haute-Savoie. Alpine areas are considerably more expensive than other parts of rural France.

84 / Buying Abroad: A Country-by-Country Guide

It is possible to buy a home that is near to both the coast and a ski resort although it may mean several hours of driving to reach both — double that in the peak season. But for the serious skier who also likes the outdoor life in summer (the Alps are not just for skiers but also walkers in the months when there is no snow) there is a range of resorts. Although there are a few ski resorts in the Pyrénées the main ones are in the Alps; the Savoie and Dauphine regions being the most expensive. More affordable are homes in the Hautes-Alpes and the Alpes du Sud.

The airports for this region are Grenoble and Geneva. The most fashionable places for those wanting to live in a ski resort include Val-d'Isère, Chamonix, Megève and Meribel. Examples of prices include lake edge apartments on Lake Geneva from £65,000 and studios to sleep four from £50,000 in La Plagne. If you are prepared to live further away from the fashionable ski resorts prices will be cheaper.

Prices. The cheapest tumbledown farm (almost little better than two barns) in the Haute-Savoie is £50,000 if you can find one. That gives an indication of prices in this area. Likewise a rabbit hutch apartment starts at £35,000. Chalets in the lesser known resorts start at £80,000. Megève is more expensive even than Chamonix, and Val-d'Isère will be above that along with Meribel. Some 2000km from the Côte d'Azur, the Briançon area is less expensive. Prices are in the medium range. In Courchevel, studios (the sort where the beds fold away) start at £24,000 and chalets start at over £275,000.

The north coast

Brittany

The north-west coast — Brittany — is also popular with Britons who find it easy to reach (many also choose western Normandy for affordable cottages.) It is very similar to Cornwall with beaches in tiny, sheltered and rugged coves. The south Brittany coastline is very popular with the French for holiday homes — competing with the Mediterranean coast — and it is very pretty and warmer than northern Brittany. However, homes are more expensive particularly around Vannes and the Morbihan Gulf. The houses have their own unique style built in stone with gables.

You can take a ferry to St Malo from Portsmouth but it takes longer (9 hours) than to Le Havre (4½ hours) which makes for a long drive. Ferries from Portsmouth run overnight to St Malo as well as to Cherbourg and Caen, which allow you to rest overnight and have a shorter drive in the morning.

Rennes is the historic capital of Brittany (Bretagne) and the coastline has many fine, golden sandy beaches and a number of pretty harbours. The largest include Brest (port of war as the French know it), Lorient, St Malo (an ancient and beautiful city) and there are wonderful and historic places to visit nearby including Cançale which has oyster beds among the best in France. You may hear Breton spoken; it is much like Welsh.

Property prices in Brittany are far cheaper than the more fashionable resorts in the south of France as well as being far cheaper — less than half the price in general — of that in England.

Inland Brittany is known as the Argoat ('land of the woods') and used to be covered in forests. The countryside is often remote as more and more locals leave the land. This, in turn, is reflected in the property prices. Small, bungalow-style buildings tend to dominate the villages.

For holidaymakers Dinard, on the Emerald coast and very close to the port of St Malo, and the historic town of Dinan, inland from Dinard down the Rance river, both make a good base. And of course there is the famous Mont St Michel on the border with Normandy, with its ancient, fortified town built on a rock which is cut off by the tide. The whole granite rock, which is 80 metres high, is a magnificent site. In the middle stands a thirteenth-century Gothic church. The Mère Poulard is one of the most renowned hotels and restaurants in northern France.

Other places to look at include Vannes, La Trinité-sur-Mer, Carnac and the Quiberon peninsula.

Prices. A two-bedroom house needing renovation can be bought from as little as £12,000. The north is cheaper than the south, which has far better weather and prices 25 to 30 per cent higher to reflect this. Further south a small farm cottage can be snapped up from as little as £15,000 — but for this price the accommodation will be very basic and you are likely to have to spend a lot on refurbishment (and local French workmen can be very expensive as well as slow). Several firms of British general builders operate in the area and do well. A renovated home with three bedrooms and garden on the Côte d'Armor will cost around £70,000–£80,000.

The Vendée is like north Brittany but La Rochelle, Rochefort, Les Sables-d'Olonne are the more fashionable resorts and more expensive. Large apartments start at £75,000 in these areas. A little further down Charente Maritique provides good beaches, mild weather and decent houses for £40,000 to £50,000.

Normandy

Normandy's western parts and the Cotentin peninsula offer plenty of cottages to choose from. It is horse-breeder and cider country. The Allied wartime landings are well remembered. Stone cottages in Mayenne start at £15,000. The climate is a bit like England but hotter in summer.

The main ports are Dieppe which can be reached from Newhaven, and Cherbourg which can be reached from Southampton.

Normandy has magnificent sandy beaches with white cliffs and tiny, bustling fishing ports. It encompasses five 'départements' and is famed for its half-timbered farmhouses (similar to a Tudor style but the wooden beams are parallel) called 'colombages'. The capital is Rouen, a Gothic town which you can reach from Dieppe. Set in the Seine valley, the villages round Rouen are a good base. Normandy is divided into two: 'La Basse-Normandie' and 'La Haute-Normandie'. Normandy will appeal to those who like the rural life rather than a hot, crowded beach. To the west, granite houses take over.

Caen, the other main town, was totally destroyed during the war and has since been rebuilt. Although it has a shopping centre it may not appeal to those looking for a holiday home. The most suitable homes, for those who do not mind the rural and often remote life, are farms.

Places to visit include Honfleur, a little fishing port, Bayeux, celebrated for its tapestry, and also the popular and fashionable resort of Deauville.

Prices. Basic farmhouses can be bought for as little as £12,500 which means that a more substantial, modernised farmhouse can be bought for £40,000 upwards. Nearer the coast prices are slightly more expensive. Prices are not dissimilar to those in Brittany. Renovation costs can be very expensive so it may be better to buy a property in good condition from around £25,000 upwards or a villa from £80,000.

Pas de Calais

As the name implies it is easily accessible from the port of Calais. It is the most northerly tip of France and the surrounding countryside, tucked away from the traditional tourist routes, offers rich, rolling countryside scattered with peaceful hamlets and towns. The most famous resort is Le Touquet. There is a small airport but most people arrive by ferry at Calais or Boulogne.

Property prices have been inflated in the past by the influx of Brits buying holiday homes but they have dipped again in recent years. Again, the climate is not as good as further south and you should be prepared to enjoy the rural life as for most months of the year the beach is out of bounds. On a hot day, it is still warmer than England.

Other attractions, for some, include Euro Disney and the Parc Astérix. An added advantage is that this region is within driving distance of Paris and the Ile-de-France, which is home to many of the most beautiful and renowned cathedrals, monuments, museums and chateaux such as Versailles and Fontainebleau.

Prices. These tend to be quite low as many Brits prefer to drive further south to the Dordogne. You can therefore buy a home from around £30,000 in the Pas de Calais. From London you can get to your house in four hours via the Channel Tunnel. Some Brits even commute.

The west coast

The coastal line between Bordeaux and the Spanish border has long been a British colony, particularly around Biarritz. Aquitaine runs south of Bordeaux to the Pyrénées-Atlantiques.

This sourthern part of the western Atlantic coast is less fashionable with the British than it used to be. Prices round Bordeaux, like any major French centre, are high. The nearest airport is Bordeaux although you can take an internal flight to Biarritz-Bayonne and some charter flights from Britain.

Homes around the Arcachon Basin are popular with the residents of Bordeaux and therefore expensive but further away the most popular one-bedroom apartments can be snapped up for £32,000. Villas are generally £150,000 minimum. It is known as Les Pays Aquitaines and is surrounded by the Massif Central and the Pyrénées. Further inland is Armagnac (accessible from Toulouse) and the Basque country. It is now a less fashionable place to buy although Biarritz, St-Jean-de-Luz and Hendaye along the silver coast still attract tourists and surfers.

Prices. A two-bedroom apartment in Biarritz starts from as little as £62,000 at the bottom end of the market but most cost far more. Prices are cheaper 1½ hours' drive away in places like Mont-de-Marsan where your money will buy you a larger property.

Biarritz, St-Jean-de-Luz and Hendaye are expensive, smart resorts with even better golf courses than on the Mediterranean coast. The Pau region adjoining is also expensive partly because there are few cheap old cottages for sale. Go further inland into the Gers, and bigger properties for less money are plentiful.

Rural France

Dordogne and Charente Maritime

This area has been very fashionable with Brits looking for a holiday home in rural France. The Dordogne is situated above the Loire Valley and is in the Massif Central. It is one of the most scenic areas of France and despite its popularity remains peaceful and relaxing. However, it is amazing that it has achieved such popularity as the weather is often poor with mists and high rainfall.

In the 1980s there was a trend to buy up chateaux at London auctions for as little as £130,000. There are spectacular villages perched on high cliffs overlooking the River Dordogne. The area signifies French country life at its most delightful with numerous abbeys and chateaux. Towards the Atlantic coast to the west there is the Charente region as well as some coastal resorts in Charente Maritime.

Prices. You can still pick up an unmodernised cottage for £20,000 and other properties for £20,000–£35,000. But be warned: this area is inaccessible. You need a car.

For those living in the northern part, which is quicker to reach, prices are around £50,000. But even the French think this region is overpriced.

The Dordogne is not what it used to be as many of the run-down places have been done up and are often overpriced. Only the Brits buy up cheap properties to do them up and sell them at a profit.

Sadly, in this region — as in most of France — it is difficult nowadays to make profits in this way.

Burgundy

This has been rather neglected by British buyers except those in the know. Burgundy or Bourgogne is vast, stretching into the foothills of the Alps. Lyon is the major city while further down the Rhône valley stretch the famous vineyards. Again, depending on proximity to Lyon, sound houses cost £50,000. The French leave renovating to the British, so wrecks can be bought quite cheaply. Beaune is a medieval architectural dream and Dijon the major city to the north.

Loire Valley

Famed for its chateaux — many of them royal — this region is relatively near to Paris and the northern ports.

Again you must be interested in the rural life even though the valley is less than 200km from Paris. The countryside is flat and houses tend to be in white limestone. You can fly to Nantes but most visitors drive from the Channel ports.

Prices: Cottages start at £10,000, but at that price will require extensive, expensive renovation. A pretty village cottage can be bought for £30,000. Bigger homes, with rock-hewn cellars, come for £50,000-plus, according to agents A House In France. A small tuffeau property in the village of Brain sur Allonnes, just north of Saumur, in need of renovation, with two rooms, can be bought for around £28,600 from Properties in France.

Other rural locations include Gascony and the Midi-Pyrénées accessible from Toulouse airport, with daily flights from Heathrow and Gatwick.

Prices. These tend to be cheap with a two- to three-bedroom cottage from £12,500 to £25,000.

Urban France

Paris

Properties in the cities move quickly and are expensive. Those looking for a flat in Paris can expect to pay £125,000 minimum. However, in cities the French tend to rent and as such it has one of the lowest home ownership levels in the EU.

Types of ownership

In general you will be buying the French equivalent of a freehold property. But there are other types of ownership that you should be aware of.

Most of Europe and the United States have condominiums known as 'copropriété' in France. Purchasing these is different from the way we buy flats in Britain which are almost exclusively on a leasehold basis with the flat purchased for a set number of years. Under 'copropriété' every buyer of a flat or sometimes house on an estate or 'lotissement' co-owns the building and as such the managing agent is employed by them, not a landlord. All the owners own a share of the block that is not part of their flat — from the roof to surrounding land used by all flat owners. A 'syndicat' of owners is responsible but often appoints a professional manager known as a 'syndic'. This can cause problems if the manager is not up to the job and there can often be difficulties getting enough 'copropriétaires' to attend meetings, let alone agree on a course of action.

Rules governing your block are contained in the 'règlement de copropriété' and you should ask for a copy before buying a property on this basis. The document will tell you what you own and the proportion of the copropriété you are buying. The amount of service charge you will have to pay is based on this and the number of parts you own also dictates the number of votes you will get at 'syndicat' meetings.

Watch out for any special rules on the collection of service charges and if you are planning to let out the flat any rules covering this, or leaving the flat unoccupied for any length of time. Also watch out for water and heating charges if these are communal — you could be penalised if you only visit occasionally as you will subsidise your more permanent neighbours. And finally, be prepared for service charges to be far larger than you were told at time of purchase.

Timesharing

This is not as common as in Spain but it is still available in France. It is known as 'multipropriété' or 'spacio-temporelle' This does take the headaches out of having a holiday home that you must leave unoccupied for much of the year. However, the pitfalls of timeshare are well known and in France some older schemes do not give you ownership, just a right to occupy the flat at certain times of the year.

If you are considering this type of property check that the timeshare is covered by a new law which involves the purchase of shares known as a 'société civile' as this gives you the right to have a say in the management of your block of flats.

However, the French legal system is still not as up to date with the timeshare concept as in some other countries and things can still go very wrong. And as with co-ownership there can still be problems if other tenants fail to keep the property in good order, the management of the block is poor or the person you buy from fails to pay their share or goes bankrupt.

Joint ownership

If you cannot afford the villa of your dreams you can always buy with another family. 'Bi-propriété' means you own the right to live in the property for six months of the year. Alternatively, you could form a company to buy the property for you and each own shares. Or you could buy in joint names. However, you will still need some sort of legal document (even if you are buying with your best friend) to cover you in case your partner does not keep up with their bills, fails to maintain the property or wants to sell. Your agreement will also have to cover what will happen should one of you pass away as the French rules of succession are very different from our laws of inheritance. And remember that French law does not recognise trusts. Owners of the land registered at the Bureau des Hypothèques are considered to be the beneficial owners. Joint ownership (joint tenancy) is not common and if one owner passes away the survivor does not automatically inherit all the property. Husbands and wives who want to own a property jointly should specifically ask for this as it is not usual.

Taking up residence

If you are planning to stay in France for more than three months you should get a residence permit — carte de séjour — at the local

Préfecture de Police. European Union citizens should request a residence permit within three months of their entry into France.

This residence permit will be valid for five years initially and can then be renewed for ten-year periods thereafter. However, if you are unemployed or have no proof of an income you will only be able to renew for one year unless you can provide evidence of adequate financial resources. To get a permit you must present your passport, proof of nationality (birth certificate), two photographs and indication of activity and evidence of financial resources if you are not seeking employment or are not a dependant of such an individual. If you are planning to work in France an employment contract should also be presented.

If you are planning to set up business as a European Union citizen you will not have to present a business permit — carte de commerçant — to set up a commercial, industrial or craft business. However, for specialised and regulated activities such as financial services you will need to show that you have the required professional qualifications.

If you are planning to live in France on a permanent basis you will therefore be domiciled for tax purposes.

Buying a home: the legal requirements

In France the notary handles the conveyancing, preparing the document which will transfer the property and seeing that stamp duty and registration fees on it are paid. The notary also checks on the title, planning enquiries and ensures that any mortgages on the property are cleared on sale.

But he or she does not give pre-contract advice. Their role includes collecting taxes and dealing with all official documents. The chances are that he or she will not speak English to the degree required to explain the entire house sale process to you and the notary will probably act for both the buyer and seller, not you alone.

You cannot conduct a house purchase without a notary. They will deal with the Land Registry — the 'cadastre' which is a tax registration system to record who owns what land; and the Bureaux des Hypothèques — which deals with mortgages, rights of way and land transfers. The actual conveyancing is known as the 'acte de vente'.

You will therefore need a lawyer as well as a notary.

It is the buyer's prerogative to choose the notary. The seller can choose another one. Although the buyer has to pay the fees, if you have two notaries it does not increase your costs — they will share one fee. Sellers sometimes insert the name of their own notary in a sale contract so check this before signing. If possible pick a notary that speaks English, knows our legal system as well as the French and has handled house purchases for Brits before. Remember all legal documents have to be in French so ask for written translations before signing.

Just as at home, never allow yourself to be pressurised into committing yourself to a purchase on the spot. A 'reservation' in the case of an off-plan sale is a deposit, not a payment. It does not commit you to buy, but if you pull out you will lose this deposit (usually 2 to 5 per cent). All sales of new residential property are subject to a seven-day cooling-off period. On new developments you may be required to sign a 'contrat préliminaire' if buying from plans. Buying a new property from plans 'en état futur d'achèvement' you will be required to make payments in stages as the building is completed. You can get mortgages in France on this basis. Just as in Britain there is a similar scheme to the NHBC for newly-built properties. The law provides for guarantees for latent defects in the building for up to ten years.

Always check who is paying the agent's commission. It should be the seller but if the notary is acting as an agent you — as the purchaser — may be left to pick up the bill.

If you are buying a flat 'en copropriété' check on the service charges which can be quite high if there is a resident concierge and communal heating.

When the 'acte de vente' (deed of sale) is prepared and the notary is ready to complete you can ask a legal expert to act as power of attorney. This is recommended as documents are never finalised until actual completion and alterations are often necessary. By appointing a legal adviser these will be known to you in advance as he or she should have looked through the draft 'acte de vente' for any pitfalls such as a right of way through your garden.

Alternatively, allow a clerk in the notary's office to be your attorney as this commits the notary himself to fulfilling the transaction in accordance with the contract and does not increase fees.

Most sales of new properties are done 'en état futur d'achèvement' — with a future completion date once the building has been completed. Remember that in France the date set for you to move in — on both newly built homes and exisiting ones — is not always adhered to and you are unlikely to be able to complete the sale and move in within a few weeks.

A power of attorney must be notarised either in France or signed before a notary public here (make sure he or she affixes the Hague Convention Apostille). A power of attorney will be required for each action — one for buying, one for getting the money from your bank etc. Once you have purchased the property your ownership will be registered at the Bureau des Hypothèques.

Completion does not take place immediately as it takes around 14 days for the money to be transferred. If money is not being paid by banker's draft or notary's cheque but a personal cheque, clearance can take up to three weeks. Completion dates, as already mentioned, are not always adhered to.

How much will buying cost?

Buying and selling costs are very high compared to the UK. It costs up to £11,000 to buy an £80,000 property — up to ten times as much as at home and costs among the most expensive in Europe.

One of the biggest outgoings is stamp duty (Droits d'Enregistrement) charged at around 6 per cent. Rates vary from department to department. On new homes VAT is charged. However, VAT and stamp duty can never both be payable.

In addition you will have notarial fees. Some 2–5 per cent goes to your solicitor depending on the value of your property as the notaire is paid a set percentage of the value with slightly higher percentages for cheaper properties.

In addition there is VAT charged at 18.6 per cent on properties less than five years old being sold for the first time. This will push up the initial asking price.

The notaire will also collect a land registry fee.

Some sellers may try to get round government taxes by asking you to pay part of the price in cash and then reducing the official asking price. Although this is tempting as you will cut stamp duty it is fraud. It is a myth that every property transaction in France is done at an undervalue.

Do not forget to include the costs of connecting water, telephone, electricity and in some cases gas as well as insuring your property.

You should not be liable for the agent's commission as a buyer. But it is often added to the purchase price and may not appear as a separate item.

If you are buying a property that has a service charge any outstanding amount should be cleared by the notaire and paid to the 'copropriété'. So you should not be left with an unexpected bill.

The annual 'taxe d'habitation' is a personal tax that must be paid by the person in occupation on 1 January each year. Make sure this has been paid or else you could have the bailiffs round. There is also the 'taxe foncière' which is charged on the property and is technically apportionable on the sale.

Surveys

These are not commonly used in France as there is no such thing as a chartered surveyor. There is the 'géomètre' who measures the land and the 'expert foncier' who gives valuations. As such, sales subject to survey are unknown. However, you can get an English surveyor by asking your local adviser. This is particularly advisable when buying an older property as otherwise you will not know what bills for repairs you may face. If you are taking out a mortgage, the lender will send round a valuer but this is not a full survey.

Outgoings after purchase

Tax

Tax is never easy to deal with — even at home. But it is even more important when abroad where penalties can be more severe and language can present a major problem.

If you take up residence in France or receive an income in France — such as rents — you will be required to file a tax return — 'déclaration fiscale' with the local 'inspecteur'. As in Britain taxes include VAT (TVA), capital gains (plus-values) and income tax and stamp duty. Taxes are dealt with by the local tax office and come under the Ministère du Budget. Stamp duty and VAT are collected by the Recettes des Impôts. Opening a French bank account is advisable.

Income tax is divided between tax on earned (impôt sur le révénue) and unearned income (impôt des révénus de capitaux mobiliers).

Death duties have been replaced by inheritance tax in France, and are known as 'droits de succession'.

There are other taxes to take into account:

- Gifts tax;
- Wealth tax (impôt de la solidarité sur la fortune);
- Local and property taxes — similar to our council tax are made up of a land tax (taxe foncière) and communal tax (taxe d'habitation);
- If resident, CSG (Contribution Sociale Générale).

If you are resident in France for tax purposes you will have to pay tax on worldwide income. If not you only have to pay tax in France on income arising in France.

Residence for tax purposes is a must if you spend more than 183 days there in any 12-month period, work there (unless it is a second job) or get most of your income from France. France is covered by the Double Taxation Convention which ensures that you do not pay tax twice — at home and in France. The French tax year runs from 1 January to 31 December. A husband's tax return includes his wife and children.

France not only gives additional tax relief to those who are married (as in the UK) but also gives tax relief to those who have children. It can mean that families with five children pay half the tax of a single man. Each taxpayer gets a number by which they divide their tax.

Single people get no reduction on their taxable income (which is their gross income minus allowable reliefs and allowances). Married couples divide by two, those with one child by 2.5 and those with five children by 5.0. A further 0.5 is added to this number for each additional child thereafter. So a family with seven children can divide their taxable income by 6.

Children are those up to the age of 18 but you can also get a reduced 'quotient familial' for those unmarried and under 21, those under 25 in full-time education and those doing military service.

As in the UK, rates of tax vary on the level of income.

If your tax affairs are simple, your French is fluent and your income modest you may try and attempt your tax return yourself.

Local tax offices can be quite helpful. But language problems will mean that an accountant — particularly from a firm that can deal with both your UK and overseas income — will make life much simpler.

Tax is payable in three instalments. A third is due on 15 February; another third on 15 May and the rest at the end of year. Tax is assessed on your preceding year's earnings. The final payment at the end of the year takes into account any adjustments necessary.

UK buyers who rent out their French properties and are not resident for tax purposes in France will pay UK tax. They should keep receipts for costs incurred in renting out the property (such as agents' fees, cleaning bills and a share of the electricity/insurance/water rates and other household expenses) to deduct against their income tax on rental income. Rental income should also be declared to the French tax authorities although tax does not have to be paid twice.

Interest on bank deposits belonging to non-residents is not liable to tax in France.

Capital gains tax

It is known as the 'Taxe de Plus-Value'. Remember this tax is on the gain, not the total sale price and there are various forms of relief.

All the legal and estate agent's costs from the purchase and sale can be set against the tax — so don't forget to keep the receipts. Inflation is also taken into account and there is a relief on properties sold from the third year of ownership with 5 per cent of the net gain written off each year thereafter. A small portion is tax free.

As a UK citizen selling your holiday home in France you will have to pay UK capital gains. Again, this only applies if you have made a profit. But remember, you may make a profit in the UK if the exchange rates mean that the amount your receive in sterling is more than you paid for the property.

Where there is an evident liability on a sale it is the duty of the notaire to deduct if from the proceeds of sale and pay it over. As the French Revenue has three years in which to re-open any CGT claim you may be required to appoint an 'agent accrédité' for that period. A way round this is to apply for a dispensation before completion.

If you are liable for CGT check how the gain has been calculated. Add the costs of buying to the purchase price to calculate the start price. Then from the sale figure deduct an inflation factor, costs of any restoration work and improvements. The gain is reduced by 5 per cent for each year of ownership after the third.

The sale is only tax free after 22 years of ownership. A double tax treaty ensures that if you are a UK resident you are not taxed on the gain in both France and the UK.

VAT (TVA)

As with other taxes don't be tempted to pay cash to avoid this. For a start, if workmen do a shoddy job you will have no means of proving they undertook work for you.

The 'Taxe sur la Valeur Ajoutée' is charged on the sale price of new properties prior to completion or on the first sale to occur within five years of completion of the building work (not completion of the sale). It is included in the price. So if you sell within five years you will have to charge TVA as well and this is included in the price (not added on top). This is 20.6 per cent of the gross proceeds of the sale.

However, you only have to pay tax on the difference between the current sale price less that TVA which was paid when you bought the property. So unless you have made a vast profit TVA is likely to be small. If you are liable for TVA you will qualify for a reduced stamp duty in the five-year period from completion of the building work.

However, the fact that stamp duty is exempted on new property means that provided you do not sell your property in the five years after sale the purchase costs are far cheaper (3–3.5 per cent of the price) than that for older properties (9–13 per cent of the costs).

Inheritance tax/Death duties

This is the biggest headache for Brits buying in France because the laws are so strict and restrictive, giving children priority over the surviving spouse. The law applies even if you are not a permanent resident. It is possible to buy a home in France through a non-French company to get around the succession rules, although this needs to be planned from the beginning and not done as an afterthought.

This tax may seem irrelevant to you — particularly if you are young or are only buying a small holiday home. But it is not. The system of death duty tax in France differs widely from the UK and can cause years of headaches which make it virtually impossible for your heirs to sell the property.

If you are fiscally resident in France you will pay duty on all assets held there as well as those held outside France. Every estate in which death duties are payable in France is taxed, not just on the property value but also at a rate of 5 per cent on the gross value of the estate as an arbitrary valuation of household goods and personal effects unless a formal valuation is undertaken, usually by a notaire.

Rates of tax depend on who you leave the estate to. If it passes in part or in full to a surviving spouse there is an initial allowance of 330,000 francs. If it is passed to parents or children in the direct line the initial allowance is 300,000 francs.

The tax is levied on sums over this at a rate which starts at 5 per cent for estates worth under 50,000 francs more than the allowance. Tax rates then rise in bands of 5 or 10 per cent which depend on whether the estate is left to a surviving spouse or ascendants or descendants. Above 11,200,000 francs the rate is 40 per cent.

It is unlikely that you will have to pay more than 20 per cent which covers estates of 200,000 to 3.4 million francs in the case of a surviving spouse and 100,000 to 3.4 million francs if left to ascendants or descendants. If the estate is left to more distant relatives the rates of tax increase and the initial allowances are reduced.

Gifts tax

You cannot get round the death duties by giving your property to your children as the gifts tax follows roughly the same rules and rates as death duties. However, you can reduce the tax bill. Gifts made by those less than 65 years old qualify for a 25 per cent reduction and those made by those between 65 and 75 qualify for a 15 per cent reduction.

Local tax

There are two forms of local rates — one on the property and one on the person occupying it, known as the 'taxe d'habitation'. Allowances vary according to how old you are and how many children you have. This tax is paid in a lump sum by the occupier resident on 1 January.

Land tax

This 'taxe foncière' is payable by the owner of the property on the estimated local rateable value. It is also due on 1 January but does not apply in the first two years after completion of a new building or the restoration of a building — you will have to apply for the tax holiday. If the property is let the tax is known as the 'taxe professionnelle'.

Tax avoidance

It is possible to buy a property in France in the name of a non-French company. This can help to avoid French tax, but is becoming increasingly difficult as there are many restrictions. Even non-French companies owning property in France may be liable to annual 3 per cent tax on the value of that property. This will not apply if your company is set up in Britain and discloses the value of the property, shareholders and shareholdings. Take careful advice before undertaking a purchase through a company.

Bank accounts

It is advisable to set up a bank account in France if only to make it easier to pay bills and to ensure that your cheques are accepted (some shops are fussy about accepting foreign cheques because they face bank charges). Opening an account with a British bank in France is often the easiest way to run your affairs. However, French banking rules will still apply. You are required to declare to customs all amounts of cash in excess of FF50,000 that you bring into the country and if you deposit a large sum like this in your bank account you may have to show a customs declaration.

Under French banking law it is the words on a cheque not the figures that carry weight so if you make a mistake when writing out a cheque remember it will be for the amount shown in words. If you are not familiar with the language this could cause you problems. You cannot issue post-dated cheques. All cheques require endorsement. You are not allowed to write out a cheque if you do not have sufficient funds — which can be difficult to avoid as cheques paid into your account can take a long time to clear. If a cheque is bounced (unpaid on presentation) you are forbidden to operate a bank account for two years unless the cheque is met within a time limit of 30 days. However, it is no longer a criminal offence to issue cheques without funds to meet them. There is no need to exchange your credit cards for French ones and there can be extra benefits to keeping your UK cards such as the facility to borrow (French card bills are automatically settled from your bank account every month). And don't forget to give your UK address to the bank if you only use your French property for the odd long weekend or holiday; that way all correspondence can be sent to your home and you can deal with it quickly.

Mortgages/finance

You can borrow either from a bank or building society in Britain or from a French lending institution. If you are not planning to move to France on a permanent basis, borrowing from your existing bank or building society may be the easiest option. Most offer loans for the purchase of second homes but will often not lend as high a loan-to-value as they would on your principal home. Try to find a bank or building society that specialises in properties abroad or has an affiliation with a lender in France — that way they will not only know the French banking system but are likely to be very helpful when it comes to transferring money to the notaire. You can also get a French franc loan from a UK lender. If you have a problem raising a loan because the property in France is not considered suitable security, you can use your home in the UK as security provided your existing mortgage combined with the new loan does not exceed the value of that property. You may have to pay a slightly higher rate of interest to cover this second loan. It is best to get your finance agreed in principle before making an offer on a property. Exchange fluctuations will affect the cost of the loan if you are paying a loan in francs from a sterling income.

Your UK loan will not qualify for mortgage interest tax relief in the UK although there is some relief in France for those who are subject to French tax and who borrow from a French bank.

The Woolwich, Abbey National and Crédit Agricole are the main lenders offering mortgages to Brits buying properties in France.

Insurance

Do not forget to insure your home. You do not want the home of your dreams destroyed and not get a penny back. Also remember that French insurance companies are far more suspicious than those at home.

Your lender will probably require insurance cover. Comprehensive policies are known as 'police multirisque habitation' which covers you against fire, flood, storm damage and lightning and the contents against theft and damage. Insurance cover to protect your possessions against damage from burst pipes or floods is essential particularly if you are not there to clean up the mess.

These policies also cover you against public liability. As at home you should read the small print — or get it translated for you.

If you live in an apartment block 'copropriété' you will only need to insure your belongings and for damage you may cause to your flat, as buildings insurance will probably be included in your service charge. When you buy the property check what is covered already.

If you are buying a holiday home you must inform the insurer that the property is left unoccupied for lengthy periods. It makes the insurance policy far more expensive but if you do not disclose the full facts your policy will be void. You will only have to inform the insurer if the non-occupancy period is more than 90 days a year in general. You can either contact a local insurer or broker or arrange cover through your mortgage lender or Lloyds.

There are 'mutuelles' companies to insure your car. These are much cheaper than alternatives, but the cover is not so comprehensive and you may have to wait months to settle your claim.

As in all EU countries you are required to have insurance by law but only the basic third-party cover. This provides the absolute minimum and you should consider more than just the 'assurance obligatoire' as it does not cover luggage, the driver or even damage done while your car is parked and the culprit cannot be found. Insurers may require that you install an alarm and have your registration number marked on all windows. You may also be required to park it in a garage when not in use and remove the radio or tape deck when leaving the vehicle.

French law

If you buy a home in France it will be covered by French law as will your personal affairs if they are linked to that property. That is why you should consider making a will. This is much simpler in France where there are different types of will including one that you can write yourself. This must be in your own handwriting and signed and dated, but do not get it witnessed. Under the French rules of succession you have to leave a proportion of your estate to your descendants or ascendants. This means that if you die leaving three children they must receive three-quarters of your estate (two-thirds for two children). On the other hand, your spouse has rights to inherit only up to a quarter of your estate in life interest. This entitlement can be increased by will or donation provided it does not exceed the portion reserved for children. Although you can make your will under British law you will still have problems because all types of real property (villa, flat, land) in France (even if you are not domiciled there) must be dealt with by French law.

Other assets if you are not domiciled in France can be dealt with under British law. This is why it may be better to employ a notaire or British lawyer to help draw up a will. Buying a property in joint names ('tontine') can get round the 'réservé' rules but will not itself save death duties.

Other legal requirements you should be aware of include registering births within three days (excluding weekends and bank holidays) and deaths within 24 hours. If you like living in France so much you may want to go the whole way and obtain French citizenship by naturalisation. This can be applied for if you have lived there for at least five years.

To save on legal problems take copies of your birth, marriage (and divorce where applicable) certificates with you.

Making money out of your home

Holiday lettings are an ideal way to cover some of the overheads of running your home in France. The easiest way to do this is to let to friends and relatives. That way you will have a reduced risk of damage to the property and will know it is in safe hands. If you don't have enough contacts to provide the level of income you need or want, then you will have to consider the following:

- *Advertising in British newspapers.* The advantages are that you can vet tenants, take a deposit in advance and tell them about your home such as where the meters can be found. However, unless you have an arrangement with a local agent or the concierge or have paid someone to look after the property there will be no one to ensure the property is clean for new tenants, and that nothing is damaged or missing and that the meters are read.

    Remember, if you are planning to let the property yourself you must draw up your own agreement according to French law not British law.
- *Using the services of a French agent.* This will cost you more and you may not get tenants from Britain alone unless the agent deals with a British tour operator or advertises in the UK. The agent will charge 10–20 per cent commission. For this they should let tenants in, check the flat is clean, read meters, keep an inventory.

The agreement with the agents is known as the 'mandat de gestion'. Make sure you know what you are signing for and that you can get out of the agreement if the agent proves to be no good. Remember, even if you appoint an agent it may be a good idea to check up on him to ensure he is not charging more than he has told you and is earning his money by keeping an eye on the property and the type of tenant. Make sure that all cheques, particularly for deposits, are made payable to you where possible and not the agent.

- *Putting your property on a travel agent's books or using a letting organisation that brings property owners together.* A look in the travel pages of national newspapers will give you a good idea as to which organisations operate in your area. Travel brochures of 'gîtes' in France show that it is possible to rent out even a modest home as a holiday let.

  Make sure that the travel group or organisation that you choose has local representation otherwise you will face the same problems as with handling your own letting — no one to let tenants in or to check that they leave the place in good order. Often a smaller organisation that looks after a number of properties in your area will be the best option. If there isn't one, you could group together with other owners of holiday homes and appoint your own manager.

Tips

- To keep cleaning bills to a minimum, ask tenants to bring their own linen.
- To avoid the possibility of a large phone bill, install a phone that accepts incoming calls only or a pay phone.
- If you are letting for more than just a few weeks make sure you — or your agent — gets the tenants to sign a more formal agreement know as the 'état des lieux'.
- You are obliged to reveal your rents to both the French tax authorities and those in Britain. Contact an accountant for more advice.
- Always send legal documents or letters to anyone relating to your property by registered AR post so you can prove that they arrived at the destination.

What if I want to sell?

If you use a French agent (agent immobilier) check he is properly licensed. Watch out for VAT (TVA) on new property resales and capital gains tax on profits you make.

Driving in France

If you are intending to stay for more than three months you do not have to pay any customs duty or VAT (TVA in France) on a foreign registered car if you import it for your own use provided you are a European Union citizen. This can mean importing a car is a cheaper option. However, prices for cars vary across Europe and even with TVA you may be able to get a cheaper car on the Continent. You will then have the advantage of buying a left-hand drive vehicle which is not only easier to drive when you are on the 'wrong' or other side of the road, but will be cheaper to insure and easier to sell.

If you are taking your existing car remember that yellow lights are now illegal and that on new cars back-seat belts are required. Make sure your car meets other requirements such as a catalytic exhaust system (if manufactured after 1 January 1993).

You should exchange your domestic driving licence for a French one if you are intending to live there for more than three months by delivering your licence to the Préfecture. This becomes compulsory within a year of taking up residence. You should also register your car in France by obtaining a tax certificate confirming that VAT or customs duties are not payable.

Also get a log book — service carte grise — from the Préfecture de Police. You get this by paying a fiscal stamp of FF200 (at time of going to press), presenting your foreign registration log book, an MOT certificate — a technical inspection card if your car is more than five years old — and by showing your passport and proof of domicile.

This 'carte grise' will also enable you to get new plates made if you so wish and a road fund licence, 'vignette', from your local 'perception' which, along with your insurance attestation, should be stuck on the right-hand side of the windscreen. If you move you must notify either the préfecture, sous-préfecture or mairie. New cartes grises are needed if you change départements as are new number plates (it is an offence to run a car with its old number plates for more than three months in a new département). And remember to keep proof that you have bought your 'vignette' by looking after the receipt. These are issued in November each year and must be bought by 1 December. If you buy a second-hand car present the sales certificate and the cancelled 'carte grise' to your préfecture along with your passport. The préfecture will be able to check on outstanding hire purchase agreements.

Do not forget that an MOT — 'contrôle technique', the official control test — is required for cars over five years old and must be undertaken every five years from an authorised garage.

The rules governing who gives way when are often ignored. You should give way to cars coming from the right on to a main road. However, at roundabouts priority is often marked differently. Learn the French highway code before venturing on the road (British motoring organisations are very helpful as their guides are written in English).

Health

As an EU citizen you can use the French National Health Service (Sécurité Sociale) even when you are in France on holiday or when you are living or working there under retirement age or are in receipt of your state retirement pension.

There is also a private medical system and an intermediate system under which the state health service will pay a proportion of the costs provided you have a prior arrangement.

Obtain form E111 before leaving. This will entitle you to free treatment or sometimes total reimbursement of costs provided you limit yourself to the state health service. If you buy travel insurance this will generally provide for private or at least better facilities.

If you are working in France you will be required to join Sécurité Sociale. Pensioners should also take form E121 to prove that they are in receipt of their UK state retirement pension in the UK.

Pensions/benefits

As a result of EU agreements you are entitled to the same social security benefits as a French citizen if you work in France even though part of your working life has been spent outside France.

In the case of your retirement pension your pension will be based on the basic salary earned in your highest paid ten years of working life. In addition you should receive a reduced state pension from the UK.

Education

If you are planning to live or work in France and have school-age children you will find that there are several alternatives — educate them at boarding school in the UK; educate them at an English-speaking school in France; or enrol them in the French education system.

The French take the education of their children seriously. They start at school at age three in the 'école maternelle' and then from age five to 10 attend 'école primaire'. After that they attend 'école secondaire'. At age 18 they sit their 'baccalauréat' which is now accepted in many UK universities.

Education is free but not textbooks or stationery. It is best to enrol your children before they reach the age of eight otherwise they may have problems integrating with the other children. Children tend to adapt more quickly than adults and usually learn French fluently in less than a year if they are in full-time education. Private schools will help them learn the language so that they can then join the state system.

Utilities

You will have to pay a deposit before you are connected to the electricity supply. It is supplied by Electricité de France and the deposit is refundable in two slices at the end of five and ten years. You will need to supply a certificate from the developer to get a supply connected to a new home and when buying any property in France check on the number of sockets and how many of them are earthed. Some sockets have a timer so that even when you replace a fuse the supply does not come back on for a couple of hours. Remember this before phoning an electrician. Beware of taking British appliances to France as they may not work. Get the wiring checked out by EDF if you are buying an older property.

Gas comes either through town pipes or in containers. Bottled gas is commonly used, as the electricity supply is not always reliable.

Water is charged for by your local water company on the amount of units you consume with special rates for those with swimming pools.

You may have to wait several months to get a telephone connected so apply as soon as you have proof that you own your home. Bills are sent out every two months and you should pay promptly as there is instant cut off if you do not pay after the reminder. You can ask for your bills to be sent directly to your bank under the 'prélèvement' system so that your bills can be settled in your absence. Gas and electricity bills can also be paid by this system.

Buying a home in Italy

Italy has it all — from the mountains, ski resorts and the lakes in the north to the sunny Mediterranean in the south. You can take your pick from crowded beaches and resorts to historical towns and cities and from quiet rural retreats to seaside villas.

Wherever you choose to live you will be guaranteed the Italian way of life — excellent food and wine, friendly people with fiery temperaments, and an easy-going attitude that will either infuriate you if you want something done in a hurry or force you to relax and enjoy things at a slower pace.

There are 96 provinces making up 20 regions — Abruzzi, Basilicata (Lucania), Calabria, Campania, Emilia-Romagna, Friuli-Venezia Giulia, (Latium) Lazio, Liguria, Lombardia (Lombardy), Marche, Molise, Piemonte (Piedmont), Puglia (Apulia), Sardegna (Sardinia), Sicilia (Sicily), Toscana (Tuscany), Trentino-Alto Adige, Umbria, Val d'Aosta and Veneto.

Where to buy

Most foreigners pick Tuscany, Umbria, Marche, Latium, Lombardy, Veneto and Liguria, generally in this order. The Adriatic coast and Sardinia also have ex-pat communities as do the major northern cities. The choice will depend on price (what you can afford) and the type of lifestyle you are looking for. You can buy a villa for under £30,000 but for that price you will get little land, the property will be in poor condition and you will have to buy in a remote area.

Tuscany

The attractions of Tuscany, with its numerous unspoilt towns and villages set in beautiful, fertile countryside, offer prospective buyers a wide range of property types at prices of both ends of the spectrum. The rich and famous flock to the spectacular medieval/renaissance town of Siena, one of the most beautiful in Tuscany — and most expensive. In contrast, to the north is the largely undiscovered area of Lunigiana which is cheaper and properties to restore can be snapped up for £30,000. But there is a reason why it is less expensive — the area is isolated, it doesn't have rolling countryside because it is semi-Alpine and therefore it is not terribly popular.

Water supply should not be a problem (it can be in the rest of the country) as the north Tuscan coast has one of the best winter climates in the whole of Italy. However, that does not mean you are guaranteed a water supply to your property, particularly if it is derelict. The Tuscan coast is busy in summer but in winter and spring it can be very cold and windy. Resorts in this region tend to shut down in winter. Some of the best wines in Italy are produced here in the wine areas of Chianti, Montepulciano and Montalcino.

The Chianti region is immediately south of Florence which, along with Pisa, are the airports of the region. The Chianti region extends to Siena in the south and San Gimignano in the west and encompasses some of the prettiest countryside in Tuscany — low hills with a patchwork of vineyards, olive groves and oakwoods. To the east Montepulciano, a walled renaissance city looking out from a dominating hilltop, is a good place to look for converted farmhouses.

To the south of the famed, historical town of Siena — a Gothic masterpiece which hosts festivals in early July and mid-August with a spectacular display of medieval pageantry — the landscape differs from other areas of Tuscany with smooth, rolling hills and hilltop towns.

Other places worth looking at include Montalcino, Pienza, Montepulciano, San Gimignano and Monteriggioni. Also worth exploring are the wooded valleys of the Arno, the medieval town of Lucca, the coast at Viareggio and the mountainous Tuscan Apennines.

Prices. Tuscany tends to be far more expensive than neighbouring Umbria. This means that even a farmhouse in need of total renovation can set you back more than £100,000. A large converted five-bedroom farmhouse with 12.5 acres and a swimming pool near Siena costs around £500,000.

The northern area of Lunigiana is much cheaper and some villages have hardly changed since medieval times. A partly restored cottage in a mountain hamlet can be bought for around £30,000. This area extends from La Spezia to Parma, from the Apennine mountains to the coastal resort of Lerici, where Shelley, Byron and D H Lawrence lived. Pisa or Genoa are the nearest airports.

Umbria

To the south of Tuscany, Umbria does not have the benefit of any coasts but instead boasts rolling green countryside and Italy's third largest lake. Many of the region's towns are set on hills with breathtaking views, and you can understand why the Italians are renowned for being romantics. Towns include Perugia (the regional capital), Assisi, Spoleto and Orvieto. Lake Trasimene is to the north and it is 1½ hours' drive from Siena and 2½ hours from Rome and Florence.

Orvieto, set on the rim of an ancient volcano, is home to one of Italy's finest Gothic cathedrals and Assisi, twinned with Bethlehem and home of St Francis, is not to be missed.

Prices. A tiny house in a hamlet in need of restoration can be bought for as little as £14,000. In Casamaggiore, a recently restored house with views to Lake Trasimene with three bedrooms and a garden can be bought for £70,000. A large apartment in a restored farmhouse complete with swimming pool will cost around £75,000 furnished. Wherever you pick will be within two or three hours' drive of Rome, Pisa, Bologna and Florence airports. The Upper Tiber Valley is also popular with the British as there are many properties in need of extensive restoration. You can buy one for £50,000 and once restored it will be worth around £200,000.

Le Marche

This lies to the east of landlocked Umbria with mountains on the west and the Adriatic sea on the east. The coastline from Pesaro to San Benedetto is heavily developed but the rest of the region is largely unspoilt. The southern sector is of most interest to homebuyers and the provincial capital Ascoli Piceno has a fine thirteenth-century piazza. Amondola is a small town of great charm with a semi-colonnaded piazza and Sarnano Terme is a spa town set in the Sibbilini National Park. This area also has good skiing.

The area is less fashionable than Umbria and Tuscany and as a result the prices are far lower. It also takes longer to get to — three hours' drive from Rome — although there are weekly flights to Ancona and Pescara in the summer.

Prices. At the lower end you can still find little houses in need of repair for under £15,000. The more typical 'casa colonica' chased after in Umbria and Tuscany can be found for between £20,000 and £60,000. Larger properties start at £60,000. For a spectacular colonial villa with large gardens near the coast you will have to pay around £300,000.

Latium

The vast majority of working ex-pats in Lazio live around Rome — mainly north of the city. Properties are the second most expensive in Italy. As a result it is only worth buying here if you are planning to work in Rome.

Lombardy

With its capital Milan, it is the most expensive area in Italy in which to buy a property. The lakes favoured by Milanese are also expensive as they are weekend escapes for the wealthy.

Veneto

This is to the north-east of Italy and is the most popular tourist region in the country with Venice, Lake Garda and the treasures of Verona, Vicenza and Treviso. To the north lie the mountains and the Pre-Alps and Dolomites.

Prices. These are not cheap. Modern villas range from £150,000 upwards.

Liguria

This is reached from Genoa airport. The area stretches from the French border with soft, sandy beaches along the bay to Genoa and then towards Tuscany to the south-east the coast becomes rugged and rocky with little inlets. Away from the coast the landscape ranges from the mountain peaks of the north to the rolling hills of the countryside.

Pesto sauce is a local speciality as are fish and seafood. San Remo is a chic resort but is quite well developed. Santa Margherita is on a beautiful corner of the Riviera and has a fashionable yacht marina. Monterosso is the largest of the five 'Cinqueterre' coastal towns with a small beach and eighteenth-century monastery.

Prices. As this area is exclusive and the market is small it is difficult to judge prices. It is one of the most expensive areas of Italy. Coastal resorts such as Bordighera, Ospedaletti, San Remo and Alassio are very expensive although further inland there are small cottages for conversion. Because there tends to be nothing but very expensive coastal properties on the market few Brits have bought here.

Calabria

Isolated from the rest of Italy this is the southernmost region and has a vast coastline. It is largely undeveloped although there are some holiday homes for sale in resorts. Most fashionable is Tropea with its narrow streets and Norman cathedral. Cap Vaticano ten miles south is one of the best vantage points for the smoking volcano of Stromboli. It is now a successful tourist area. The main attraction is the warmer climate and the international market for property has yet to take off. It is one of the last undiscovered Mediterranean locations but is inaccessible. The airport at Lamezia Terme operates internationally during the summer but the rest of the year you will have to connect at Rome.

Prices: A little and remote peasant's house in need of restoration can be bought for well under £15,000. Villas finished and in good order can be anything in excess of £100,000.

Campania

The capital is Naples and it includes the islands of Ischia and Capri and the coastal resorts of Sorrento, Positano and Amalfi.

Resorts are always expensive and there is a shortage of accommodation. The Amalfi coast is one of the most picturesque in Italy and of course there are Mount Vesuvius and Pompeii to visit.

Sicily and Sardinia

The eastern half of Sicily is popular with the British particularly around the resorts of Messina and Syracusa. Many resorts have become high-rise jungles. In the past newspaper stories of Mafia connections may have deterred buyers, but it is safe to live there. However, watch out for the high cost of living.

Sardinia is a popular and exclusive tourist island. Costa Smeralda is probably the best place to look but it is the most expensive.

Prices. Prices in Sardinia's Costa Smeralda start at around £100,000 and for £250,000 you can get a three-bedroom villa with large garden and sea view.

In Sicily apartments in a residence with swimming pool and tennis court start at around £130,000.

Elba

Off the Tuscan coast, Elba is reached by ferry (a 50 minute journey from Piombino and Livorno) and is the third largest Italian island. It is mountainous and has rich woodland as well as Mediterranean brush. Fine sandy beaches and rocky coves and inlets and crystal-clear water make it an ideal summer location.

Prices. Apartments start at £50,000 and villas at £270,000.

Buying a property

Unlike the Mediterranean resorts of Spain and France, the property market tends to be aimed at Italians. Therefore you will find advice harder to come by.

Employ a local surveyor (geometra) to help you with searches.

Always check at the local Land Registry (Ufficio Tecnico Erariale) and the Deeds Registry (Conservatoria dei Registri Immobiliari) as well as the local municipality (comune) to check that the seller has a registered title to the property. Also check that there are no outstanding mortgages or loans charged against the property.

Make sure planning permissions have been obtained and building regulations complied with as well as municipal taxes paid.

Sales contracts (contratto preliminare or compromesso) are not always drawn up by lawyers but often by the vendor or his agent. This is a legally binding contract. You will usually have to pay a deposit of at least 10 per cent which is non-returnable, so it is best to get your lawyer (avvocato) to help in drawing up the contract so you can insert your own conditions.

The deposit, 'caparra', should be paid to the vendor or to the notary (notaio). If the seller breaks the deal, you get back twice the amount you paid in deposit. If you fail to complete you will lose your deposit. After this has been signed the final deed then transfers ownership. This is the 'atto di compravendita' or 'rogito notarile'.

As with other European countries a notaio will oversee the conveyancing. But remember he will not be acting for you so you should get your own avvocato as well as surveyor. The notaio will work for both sides. You can choose the one you want to use.

The notaio will draw up the deed, see that any capital gains tax has been paid and then register the document.

The deed will include a description of the property, its boundaries, price, map reference and the receipt for the purchase money. The conveyance document also includes details of rights of way and confirms that the property is sold with vacant possession and that it is not subject to any charges.

Get documents translated and try to get advisers who can speak English. You can also employ a 'commercialista' (a combination of accountant and lawyer) in addition to an avvocato to help you with advice on legal and tax matters.

How much will it cost?

It will cost approximately £6000 to buy an £80,000 property but allow for at least 10 per cent above this estimate.

Taxes include government tax, registration and mortgage tax. Tax is paid on the increased value of the property. This capital gains tax is known as the INVIM, but it is being phased out and will disappear at the end of the year 2002. Anyone buying a property now will be subject to the new system — ICI — which will value the property based on a set formula, taking into account the local rate and the cadastral value. Under the old system, the price is often under-declared to reduce the tax. But as long as the price declared matches or exceeds the official value based on a notional annual rent, the 'rendita catastale', it is allowed.

Although there is a tax allowance (currently 200,000 Lire) it does not apply to foreign buyers.

In addition there is the registration tax. First-time buyers in Italy get a reduced rate of 5 per cent instead of the set 11 per cent figure.

VAT is paid on purchases of new homes. This is currently 19 per cent (reduced to 4 per cent for a non-luxury building). The purchaser is also liable for the notaio's fees.

If you cannot be present at the signature of the documents you can appoint an attorney. Ask at an Italian Consulate for a form. If you appoint power of attorney or attend in person you will need your passport, birth and marriage certificates.

You can buy property through a UK company to save on death duties. But you may be required to sell to foreigners only. Any property registered in the name of a company may still be liable to capital gains tax.

Running costs

If you are buying a property in a complex or an apartment you will pay service charges. If you are away from the property for weeks on end, try to pick somewhere with a resident concierge. It will be more expensive, but could save you money and heartache in the long run.

You may also have to pay local taxes (see below).

Taxes

This may seem a bit of a joke in a country where tax evasion is reputed to be common. It is up to you to declare your taxes and once in the system you cannot escape.

If you are going to be a resident in Italy a 'codice fiscale' or tax number is needed as you will have to produce it when buying a car or even paying your bills. You do not have to make a declaration if you have no income or your income is a state pension. Once you are in the tax system and after paying your first year's tax you will automatically become liable in the following November for 95 per cent of the tax paid in the previous year unless you have not earned the same amount. Your best bet is to consult a 'commercialista' to help. Italy has a tax treaty with the UK which means you should not pay tax twice on the same income.

IVA

The Italian VAT has a range of tax rates depending on the item. So on some luxury items you may be paying 30 per cent but on food only 3 per cent.

First-time buyers taking up residence in Italy pay IVA at only 4 per cent on the property. Otherwise it is 10 per cent plus 750,000 Lire for stamp duty.

INVIM

This is the 'Imposta sugli Incrementi di Valore degli Immobili' — a form of capital gains tax. However, it was abolished on 31 December 1992 but if you bought a property before that date you will still be eligible to pay it until January 2002, should you sell. It has been replaced by ICI.

ICI

'Imposta Comunale Immobili' is the tax that replaced capital gains tax (INVIM) and the local income tax (ILOR) which was previously applicable to income from property.

Paid annually at a rate established by local authorities, ICI is levied at a level between 0.04 and 0.07 per cent based — not on the market value of the property — but on the catastal value (something that originated in Napoleonic times and has become a public general list held by the local Land Registry. All properties are listed with the territory divided in accordance with the jurisdiction of a local authority).

ICI is similar to council tax in the UK and is payable by owners of flats, buildings, building or agricultural land in Italy. In addition to the owners, other persons such as a beneficiary having a life interest are also charged. Due in two annual instalments (45 per cent paid between 1 and 30 June each year and the remainder by 20 December), it is paid at the post office. Mountain/hill land listed by law is exempted, as are certain farm buildings and land.

IRPEF

'Imposta sul Reddito delle Pesone Fisiche' is the Italian income tax. Non-residents are taxed on the local income produced in Italy net of some allowances. Income from properties, interest from bank accounts, dividends from companies and income from employment are all subject to income tax. If income is in excess of 360,000 Lire you have to file a tax return every year. If you fail to do so you will be unable to sell your property. Some people have been caught out by making such a simple mistake. Income net of Italian taxes may be subject to UK tax. But remember, under the Avoidance of Double Taxation treaty you will be able to deduct the tax paid in Italy from any income tax due in the UK. Tax rates vary between 10 and 51 per cent. The tax return you need is Form 740. You can organise this from England through a professional based in Italy.

Be warned that it is possible to have an income from property even if the flat/house is unoccupied. This is due to the fact that taxable income from land is calculated on the rateable income and this is the average ordinary income which the law assumes can be produced by the particular property. This is the 'rendita catastale'. It must be declared in a tax return even if no money is actually received. However, you can deduct a percentage of mortgage interest provided, as a non-resident, your Italian home was your main residence.

Refuse collection tax

Known as 'Tassa Smaltimento Rifiuti' this is related to the costs of refuse collection for Italian properties. There are reductions/exemptions for non-residents or for properties other than the main residence. Unoccupied residences are exempted. You must lodge your change of ownership to qualify for a reduction.

TV licences

If you import a television you must have proof that you have bought one of these which can be payable three monthly, six monthly or yearly. Few Italians cheat on this tax — partly because the fines are enormous.

Utilities

ENEL, the electricity company, the gas company and the water company, which is usually in country districts, must all be given plenty of notice before you move in.

Water from the local 'comune' or local 'Societa d'Acquedotto' is on a metered basis. If you have more than 1000 square metres of land you will need a second contract. You cannot use your basic water supply for watering the garden unless it is very small.

You will be given a water allowance up to a certain limit and over that you will pay penal rates. You should consider a reserve tank or even a reservoir and install a pump otherwise you may not have enough water or water pressure to heat the water. Remember to lag pipes if you are living in a part of Italy that gets cold in winter.

Gas

Most of the larger towns have gas so gas central heating is possible provided gas appliances are approved and fitted by the local gas authority. In rural areas bottled gas is widely used. You can have a holding tank known as a 'bombolone'.

Electricity

If you are buying a cottage in a rural area you may have to generate your own electricity, otherwise ENEL will supply. ENEL will carry out an inspection. You may be better off getting a residence contract rather than one for non-residents.

Telephones

Again, residents pay less than non-residents and to get the better deal a residence certificate must be produced. You may be required to purchase your fax machine from the main telephone company, Telecom Italia.

Rubbish

You are usually required to take your rubbish to a central container as there are few door-to-door collections.

Bills

It is advisable to pay on banker's order so you do not run the risk of getting cut off. There can be substantial fines and a long delay if you want the service reconnected.

Renovating a property

Planning permission takes on average about three months to obtain. If you buy a property with consent check with the 'comune' concerned. Remember that builders tend to try and avoid VAT but if you do not pay the full amount you may have trouble getting redress if their work is shoddy.

You will not be able to improve your property by increasing its size, changing its building line, its windows and in certain tourist areas its colour, without permission. Once this has been obtained from the 'comune', Provincia or in larger matters the Region, it must be taken to the 'municipio' to get the licence before you begin work. Swimming pools also need permission and special arrangements must be made regarding drainage.

Remember it can be more expensive to renovate a house than to build from scratch. Central heating and modern bathrooms cost a lot. Water can be rationed so you may need to install an underground tank and you may have to pay a hefty bill for connection to the electricity supply. Then of course there are plumbing costs and central heating installation expenses.

Wood-burning stoves are a good idea if you have easy access to wood. There are also rules on ceiling heights (2.75 metres minimum) and you may find that your cheap ruin turns out to be very expensive when you have to raise ceilings or dig down to increase ceiling heights.

If you are worried about planning permission you can sign a contract with the provision that it is granted. Register your building contracts and include penalty clauses. And pay the full price including VAT to save later on when it comes to capital gains as these costs are deductible.

Raising finance

Mortgages in lire are a big risk not only because of exchange fluctuations but also because interest rates rise and fall so rapidly. If your income is in sterling, get a sterling loan.

However, if you are working in Italy and get your income in lire you may be better off taking out a lire mortgage. Because of exchange fluctuations you will probably only be able to borrow half the value of the property. The Abbey National and Woolwich both lend on properties in Italy.

Make sure your bank registers the fact that your money has been brought in from abroad as it may be difficult to transfer the money back out at a later date.

Residence permits

As an EU citizen you have free entry into Italy but you must obtain a residence permit within three days of arrival if you are planning to live there. This is valid for one year and renewable annually and is available from your local 'municipio'. For full-time permanent residence, a certificate of residence is needed to make you subject to Italian laws and taxes. You will not need a work permit.

Inheritance

Warning. As in much of Europe, the Italian law on inheritance stipulates that a minimum portion of the estate is passed on to your children.

As a foreigner purchasing a property in Italy you do not need to worry about Italian inheritance laws provided you make a will. Under Italian law the contents of a foreigner's will are governed by the law of nationality but that does not mean you can always escape death duties.

Identity cards

If you move to Italy you should get an Italian identity card which will state your nationality. You should carry it with you and it is much easier than carrying your passport.

Moving in

If you take any of your furniture and personal effects into Italy you must give a list of the items to your nearest Italian Consulate which will stamp the list 'visto'. Your furniture will have to clear customs and to simplify this it may be best to use an Italian customs clearing agent at the frontier where your goods will arrive unless your removal firm is also a customs clearing agent. You should also present proof that you have purchased a home. Importing furniture should be free of VAT provided items are brought into Italy within six months of having taken up residence.

You can take your television with you as Italy uses the same system as the UK.

Health

Quite a number of doctors speak English because they have done postgraduate work here or in the US. But the public health service may not be of a sufficient standard so you are advised to take out private health insurance. For details of social security rights contact the DSS before leaving.

British citizens should get form E111 from the DSS if they are going to Italy for short periods. This will give them the same benefits as are available to Italians in Italy.

If you stay for more than three months you can renew by post, but you may still be required to pay some contributions. This form will not cover repatriation to the UK if you are seriously ill. If you stay in Italy for any length of time you can join the Italian health scheme by paying a proportion of your taxable income, but a private health policy may still be a safer option.

Insurance

If you insure your property with a company outside Italy you will have to pay a tax on your policy above that charged on local policies. But you may get a better service and it will cover more events.

Be warned: Italian insurers may sign you up for ten years and you may not be able to cancel.

Car insurance must cover at least third party, fire and theft and to obtain comprehensive cover you must get an additional policy. Again watch out for how long you are buying the policy for.

Pensions

Contact the DSS at Newcastle before leaving. You will then get your pension, free treatment and free medicines. Your pension can be paid to you in Italy.

Buying a home in Portugal

Portugal is on the south-western tip of the European mainland but, unlike other resorts where Brits buy homes, is on the Atlantic coast not the Mediterranean.

Since the revolution of 1974 which overthrew 50 years of virtual dictatorship much of the country has been 'discovered' and there are now many overdeveloped resorts. Most of the Brits tend to congregate in the Algarve, but there are other coastal regions which are worth considering. Much of the country remains unspoilt and there are still deserted beaches to be found.

Even before Portugal became a member of the European Economic Community in January 1986 there was already a thriving ex-pat community. But since then there have been a number of changes — most notably an increase in prices and the appearance of foreign goods on supermarket shelves.

Although the country has progressed, you must get used to the slower pace of life. This may be something you are yearning for, but it can be infuriating when you want something done — and now.

Portugal is only 35,500 square miles — smaller than the UK and a sixth of the Iberian Peninsula.

Even within the small land area there is a variety of terrain, from ski slopes to citrus groves, from fishing villages to rice paddies and from sandy beaches with large tourist resorts to sleepy little towns with whitewashed cottages.

But for most Brits looking to buy a home, the 500 mile coastline is the main attraction — particularly the Algarve to the south which is far warmer than the northern coast which can have cold winters. Even in these tourist areas life can be very quiet out of season so look for somewhere near a busy town so that you are not totally isolated in the early spring or autumn.

The other area of appeal to foreigners is the Estoril coast in the lower part of Estremadura which also has the attraction of being near

Lisbon. Oporto, famed for its port wine industry, tends to be for the Brits who work in Portugal.

Then there are the islands — Madeira 500 miles south of Lisbon off the coast of Morocco and the Azores which are in fact mid-Atlantic.

Less popular with the Brits are the northern regions but if you do not mind cold winters and like the outdoor life there is Minho in the north left-hand corner which produces wine and has many trout-filled rivers. The north-eastern province of Tras-os-Montes is even more isolated and untouched by tourism.

The central part of Portugal takes in the southern part of Beira Litoral as well as the province of Estremadura in the west and Beira Baiza and Ribatejo. Coimbra is probably the best known city in this area. On the banks of the Mondego river, it is historic and full of life. On the coast of Estremadura the climate is warm and there are good beaches as well as flights to Lisbon. Sintra is where the Portuguese royals used to spend the summer.

Here there are real gems — Estoril and Cascais which is like the south of France with casinos, expensive hotels and large villas. Across the estuary from the Portuguese Riviera is Palmeal, a pretty town with an imposing castle.

The southern zone is made up of the lower part of Alto Alentejo, Baixa Alentejo and over the mountains the Algarve — the greatest attraction of this area. The southern coast — 100 miles from Cape St Vincent to the Guadiana river and to Spain — has varying landscapes and climates. The east is warmer than the west where Atlantic winds prevail.

The Algarve

This is split into three main areas. The *Western Algarve* between Cape St Vincent and Albufeira includes the towns of Lagos and Portimao. Albufeira, to the west of Faro, is the most popular destination for holidaymakers. This was originally a fishing town with a large open-air market with unique charm but has now become more commercial with bustling streets, noisy nightclubs and busy restaurants. Further along Lagos is an important agricultural market town and Portimao is a large fishing port and a popular destination for families. Expats tend to buy in Praia da Rocha and Carvoeiro as well as Luz Bay, Armacao de Pera and Praia da Gale.

The *Central Algarve* stretches from Albufeira to Faro, offering a wide choice of property at varying price bands. In this area Vilamoura (with its marina), Quinta do Lago and Vale do Lobo are the major exclusive resorts with some very expensive villas. In fact, the area of golf courses near Val do Lobo/Quinta do Lago is so expensive (a good three-bedroom villa will cost at least £200,000) it is known as the golden triangle.

The *Eastern Algarve* between Faro and Vila Real de Santo Antonio and the Spanish border is much quieter with fishing communities and farmlands. There is less development because of regulations to prevent construction between the main coastal road and the sea.

Remember, if you are buying in a holiday resort it is likely to be almost deserted out of season. So if you want to visit at these times you may find that the bustling local bar is shut, as are the restaurants. And you will have to spend most of your time battling with other British and European tourists in the summer when the Algarve gets very crowded. That is why it is best to visit at several times of the year to make sure that your home is ideal for more than a couple of weeks a year in early and late season. However, if you are buying a holiday home a tourist area will be ideal — particularly if you want to let it out. However, if you are only going to visit occasionally it may be cheaper to rent than buy.

Prices. Anything on the coast and in a major tourist area is expensive and you will have to pay a premium for the sort of services you expect. Even if you are connected to the electricity and water supply it can get cut off. Watch out for homes that seem cool and relaxing in summer but are cold and damp in winter.

Developments are known as 'urbinization'. Timeshares are also quite common. Apartments are restricted to the major towns and tourist resorts.

You can also opt for a run-down ruin of a farmhouse and do it up (a peculiarly British pastime). These start at around £15,000–£20,000 in a 'peaceful' (ie remote) area with no mains water supply or electricity and in need of renovation. But the costs of improving a home (unless you are a builder) and the language problems in employing someone else to do it for you may mean that this is not worthwhile.

On the western side of the south coast near Lagos a luxury villa with five bedrooms and pool can be bought for £270,000. A smaller villa — but still with three bedrooms — on a sought-after golf complex such as Val do Lobo in the Algarve, can be bought from £200,000 upwards and a small two-bedroom villa in the same resort for £75,000 upwards. For a three-bedroom villa only a little further away from the golf course prices drop to £130,000–£160,000.

A typical Algarvian house slightly away from the beach near Faro can cost £50,000 restored — but there will not be a pool, although if you are lucky electricity will be connected. In the most popular coastal areas you will get little more than a very small apartment for £40,000. Away from the Algarve Cascais is probably one of the most expensive resorts.

For larger properties on some of the luxury resorts you will almost have to be a millionaire but for this you will get a lifestyle to match with maid's quarters, swimming pools, more bedrooms and bathrooms than you can fill and of course access to local facilities — golf, horse riding and the top restaurants.

Prices have started to recover although there is still a great deal of property around. A new way of buying is shared ownership — not timeshare — with four families buying 13 weeks' use each.

Flights: Faro for the Algarve and Lisbon for resorts further north.

How to buy a property

Estate agents (mediador autorizado) must be registered. Although this does not mean that they are approved, a licence is required to sell property in Portugal. A list of Portuguese agents may be obtained from the Portuguese Chamber of Commerce.

As in most of Europe you will require two legal advisers — an 'advogado' who is your counselling lawyer and the 'notario' or notary who handles the conveyancing. You have to use a notary for all property transactions and although the 'advogado' is not essential, you should employ one.

Do not sign documents before you have sought legal advice and insist on a translation. It is better not to use the same lawyer as the vendor.

All stages of the homebuying process involve the signing of documents in Portuguese. Some developers will ask you to sign an option or contract of reservation and to pay a nominal deposit. Private individuals may not insist on this. Signing one of these documents is safe provided you check that the deposit is returnable if you do not proceed and the document is subject to title and planning searches.

Your legal adviser should then make Land Registry and municipal authority searches to check that:

- the vendor has registered title to the property. If the title is not registered, there can be risks;
- there are no mortgages or other charges on the property. If it is not free of charges ('livre de onus') it may be unsafe to buy;
- there is a certificate of habitation. All properties must have one of these, which are granted by the town hall, and must be handed over by the vendor or builder upon sale and may also be required before the Electricity Board will connect you;
- planning consents have been obtained and complied with. For your own safety also ensure that building regulations have been met. You can enquire at the same time about any plans for future development;
- confirm that the vendor is up to date with municipal taxes.

Surveys

As in many other European countries structural surveys are not common but you will need to get the property valued if you are planning to take out a mortgage. If you are buying an older property you can either get a survey or employ an architect or builder to tell you what the approximate costs of renovating the property may be.

Flats and apartments or villas in estates

If you are not buying a property freehold or it is on a communal complex you should obtain a copy of co-ownership rules, the latest accounts of the community owners and a statement of the vendor's balance of account with the community in case there are any outstanding payments.

Contracts

After completing searches you will then have to sign the first contract. Known as the 'Contrato Promessa de Compra e Venda' this first promissory contract is equivalent to exchange of contracts. At this stage you do need to use a notary but remember that the promissory contract is a legally binding commitment to buy on the terms stated.

Notarial authentication of the signatures is quite common and this is recommended if you are buying an uncompleted unit.

This document will contain details of the property including price and the names of the parties involved and any special conditions. At this stage you will have to pay at least 10 per cent of the purchase price but developers may demand more — up to 20 per cent. Check that the balance is to be paid on receipt of the title deeds (escritura).

If you are making stage payments during the building of the development make sure that the vendor is solvent and the building programme either bonded or properly funded.

Check what services are included. The costs of connecting water, gas and electricity should be included in the price.

If the vendor pulls out of the deal they will have to pay you double the deposit. However, if the buyer reneges he loses only his deposit and all other monies paid to the builder or vendor.

For extra protection you can demand that future transfer of the property is registered prior to the final Deed of Conveyance. This will require a notary and you may have to pay a higher deposit.

Completion

This is on the date set in the promissory contract or can be linked to the completion of construction. You are at risk until a formal document transfers ownership into your name. This is known as the 'Escritura Publica de Compra e Venda' and has to be prepared and witnessed by the notary who will need the habitation licence (applying to all property built after 1951) and the tax registration card (caderneta predial) for the property. The 'escritura' is then registered in the Land Registry and Inland Revenue.

Your certified copy, the title deed, is a fuller document than the promissory contract and will describe not only the parties involved and the property but also list rights of way and use, boundaries, location within a development, size and make-up of the unit, price, method of payment and any special conditions. Most importantly it should contain a statement/warranty that the vendor is the legal owner of the property, that it is sold with vacant possession and is not subject to any charges. Because of these risks between the promissory contract and final escritura you should not delay at this stage.

You will then have to get your title deed registered at the relevant registry. The notary will only do this if you instruct him to do so and it can take up to a year.

When you set up a bank account to transfer funds into Portugal ask your lawyer or the bank for the requirements you need to meet to import money for house purchase so that you can then easily take the money out when you sell. A non-resident escudo account will be best.

How much will it cost?

Most costs must be borne by the purchaser, and are among the highest in the EU, adding between 12 and 20 per cent to the purchase price.

Transfer Tax — known as SISA — is paid at varying rates depending upon the price of the property. There is an exemption on the cheapest homes but most homebuyers will pay around 10 per cent of the purchase price. Under-declaration of the property value in order to save on tax is quite common but, be warned, the authorities have been clamping down on tax avoidance and, in the long run, this could lead to a higher capital gains tax liability. And, watch out, the local tax office assesses the value on an independent basis to catch those trying to reduce their tax liability. The tax is declared to the local tax office 'Reparticao de Financas' and is paid before completion of purchase. However, if the purchase does not go through, you can apply for a repayment.

Notarial fees and land registry fees: these can add up to between 2 and 4 per cent.

VAT: may be payable on building contracts.

Your own legal fees and translations must be added to the above.

Costs after you buy

If you have bought a condominium or a home on an estate you will have to pay maintenance and repair bills and service charges if you have bought a flat. You will also have to pay gas, water, electricity and telephone charges as well as insurance.

Municipal taxes must also be paid (these are between 1.1 and 1.3 per cent of the value and are paid annually but urban homes, unless they are very expensive, are usually exempt for ten years) along with income tax if you let your property. Every buyer must obtain a taxpayer number.

You are advised to open a local bank account to meet these payments promptly.

And do not forget removal costs. Personal effects may be imported free of duty if you have owned them for more than 12 months. Household goods need a 'residencia' or 'escritura' if they are to be imported duty free.

Services/utilities

If you live away from a tourist resort you will probably have to take your rubbish to the local collection box or 'lixo' box. Drainage is likely to be a cesspool or 'fossa' and you will probably have to generate your own electricity and have water pumped up or stored in a cistern. If you do not invest in central heating, an open fire or wood-burning stove is a must as it can get chilly in the winter, even in the Algarve. The only mains gas supply is in Lisbon. Telephones tend to be expensive and you may face delays in getting one connected. Bills are issued monthly and need to be paid on time. Electricity supply is 220 volts, which means you can take your UK appliances with you (but not your television). If you have mains electricity, get a meter fitted outside your home so that the meter can be easily read (a must if you are absent for many months of the year). If not you will have to fill in a form — remember, all bills must be paid monthly and on time.

Renovating a property

This is never cheap — even at home. Make sure that you have planning permission if you are planning to build a new property. Portugal has implemented a regional plan for the Algarve, the PROTAL, which limits uncontrolled development and new building is restricted. VAT is charged on building contracts. Even minor alterations may need planning permission, so check with the town hall before starting work.

What if I want to sell?

The vendor pays the estate agent's costs, as in the UK. Make sure your agent is properly licensed. Commissions range from 4 to 10 per cent.

To take the proceeds of sale out of Portugal you will need your original import licence (BAICP) which proves your original investment came from outside Portugal.

Your profit on sale will be liable to Portuguese capital gains tax. Half of the total profit is liable but this is corrected by an annual inflation allowance. If you are a UK resident you will also be liable to UK capital gains tax but the amount paid in Portugal is allowed as a credit against the UK tax.

Taxes

In addition to the transfer tax on purchase, municipal taxes and a potential capital gains tax liability, you should also note that if you live in Portugal for over 183 days in any one year you are treated as a resident and are liable to Portuguese income tax on your worldwide income (payable at between 15 and 40 per cent). Residence permits should be applied for before arrival at a Portuguese Consulate. Non-residents pay tax only on any income they receive in Portugal. You should apply for your fiscal number on arrival. You may need a tax card before you buy a house or apartment. It is obtained by completing a form and submitting a photocopy of the first five pages of your passport (last two pages if you have a new EU passport) to the local tax office in the area of residence. You may also be required to deduct income tax at the basic rate of tax from interest payments to a foreign bank and pay this to the Inland Revenue in the UK. The rate can be reduced to 10 per cent under the UK/Portugal tax treaty.

Death duties: are payable on a rate varying from 4 to 50 per cent depending on the relationship with the beneficiary and the value of the estate.

The Portuguese tax year is the calendar year and tax returns must be filed by 15 March if you are resident in Portugal for tax purposes.

If you open a deposit account in Portugal you will receive interest after 20 per cent deduction of tax — this is not taxed again.

Driving

You can take a foreign registered car to Portugal for up to six months on production of the registration document and you are advised to get a Green Card insurance document from your insurer.

If you are planning to stay for more than 185 days a year you should re-register it under Portuguese plates which will be exempt from tax if you have owned it for more than six months prior to applying for residence.

You can drive on your existing driving licence for one year but after that should apply for a Portuguese driving licence with your identity card, 'bilgete de identidate', foreign driving licence, two photographs, proof of medical examination and fee.

Health

There are many English-speaking doctors and free emergency out-patient treatment is available to you on production of a British passport. If you are travelling to Portugal on holiday your travel insurance policy will cover you for some private health care. Health treatment is free on production of a British passport and DSS certificate E111. For more permanent stays you should take out private health insurance. Also contact the DSS for pamphlet SA29 to find out your rights with respect to the state health system.

Importing goods

If you want to bring in furnishings and general belongings a baggage certificate is required and is obtained by proving that your usual residence for the last year has been outside Portugal. You will have to list what you want to import, declare that you have owned the items for at least six months and say that you own a home in Portugal, usually with a copy of the escritura.

Pets can be brought into Portugal fairly easily provided you have a certificate of good health from your vet, an export certificate from the Ministry of Agriculture, Fisheries and Food and your pet has been inoculated against distemper and rabies.

Residence permits and identity cards

You will need to apply for a residence permit within three months if you want to live in Portugal. If you are planning to retire to Portugal you should apply to the Immigration Office, the 'Servico de Estrangeirors e Fronteiras'.

After being resident for six months you should obtain a foreigner's blue identity card. For this you will need a certificate from the British Consulate certifying your identity and a document from the Immigration Department declaring that you are legally resident. EU citizens do not require work permits.

Wills

Even if you are not resident in Portugal for tax purposes you should make a Portuguese will covering your assets there and get it signed in the presence of a notary and two witnesses. Name an executor resident in Portugal for ease in administering the estate. Although a will made in the UK is valid in Portugal a Portuguese notarial will simplifies the administration of the estate and saves costs. Make sure that your two wills do not conflict.

Language

Unless you are living in Lisbon, Oporto or in the heart of a busy town in the Algarve such as Albufeira, you may find it hard to communicate with the locals. This could cause major problems if you are trying to get the plumbing fixed or order an item for your home. Portuguese is not an easy language to learn but you should try to learn at least a few important words. An easy way is to watch television are there are many British and American films with Portuguese subtitles.

Buying a home in Greece

Greece, which occupies the southern part of the Balkan peninsula, is made up of the mainland plus many large and small islands. To the east is the Aegean sea, to the west the Ionian and to the south the Mediterranean. Greece splits into the Ionian Islands, the most popular being Corfu, the Peloponnese, the Aegean Islands which include Rhodes, Crete, and on the mainland Thrace, Macedonia with Thessaloniki as the major city, Thessaly, Epirus and central Greece with Athens the capital city.

Nowhere in Greece is more than 100km from the coast and there are some 8332 miles of broken coastline. The huge range of islands — there are 427 of which 134 are inhabited — means you can take your pick when it comes to lifestyle: either a bustling port, a remote hilltop or a modern resort.

The main attraction is the weather. Greece has virtually no rain in summer, the seasons are mild and there is often a cooling breeze. The different geography of islands means that temperatures and rainfall will differ but one thing you are guaranteed is sun.

The north-west is Alpine while parts of Crete border on the subtropical. The large central plain has high summer temperatures and obtaining fresh water is often a problem. Average daily temperatures are well into the 80s during the peak season.

The most popular islands are Crete, Rhodes and Corfu. Other islands within a short sailing distance of the Piraeus port in Athens have become popular with tourists but transfer times by ferry may mean that these will feel too remote, especially in low season and often you have to connect to ferries by a night flight making the journey tiring and slow. So you will probably prefer to pick an island with direct flights or flights you can connect to from the mainland.

Greece has 444 ports of which 123 are large enough to handle passenger or freight traffic. Of the 37 civilian airports in Greece, two-thirds are located on the islands.

Some 1.6 million Brits take their holidays in Greece each year. Since Greece became part of the EU, foreign nationals have been able to buy properties in Greece with a little more ease. But you will be required to fill out a declaration (the 'Pothen Esches') stating where you got the money from to buy the property. This is to clamp down on tax evasion (see below).

Prices. Properties are now valued by a district valuer who bases the price on the rateable value. However, properties may be sold for more than this and the true price should be declared (despite any pressure to the contrary from the vendor who may want to reduce his tax liability on the sale).

It is hard to generalise about property markets and prices because Greece is so fragmented. The geology, climate, local economy and type and availability of properties vary from island to island and region to region.

On the mainland the northern provinces around Thessaloniki villages tend to be picturesque but property supply is low. But anywhere near the coast and on an island will be more expensive. Even on Naxos, one of the more southerly islands, a three-bedroom town house with a guest apartment is £130,000. However, away from the tourist track a two-bedroom villa on the mainland in Zante (6km from the airport) will cost around £68,000 fully furnished.

An example of how prices compare depending on location is: a traditional detached stone-built house in a village on Rhodes with two double bedrooms and roof garden costing £63,000; a detached stone house in Messinia, in the Peloponnese in need of renovation (including bathroom) for £23,250; and, a restored old town house on Poros for £110,000.

On the sparsely populated Peloponnese, in Portoheli, a sheltered bay and fishing village which has become a seaside resort in recent years and is linked to Piraeus by hydrofoil, a two-bedroom apartment with a quarter of an acre will cost around £58,000. A one-bedroom detached villa with a mooring on the canal will cost around £70,000. On Spetses a one-bedroom apartment can be bought for as little as £28,000.

Demand has increased in Crete since foreigners were first allowed to invest in property in 1990. To meet this need locals are building homes that look old — with wooden ceilings, tiled roofs and solid external walls — but which also have modern plumbing, electricity, insulation and air conditioning. This has met the demands of the current market, as there are too few stone cottages in good condition for sale, but enough locally quarried stone to build new properties. Old buildings on the islands sell for £15,000 upwards and one-bedroom houses with all mod cons from £50,000 to £70,000.

However, in general you may be surprised at how high prices are in Crete. But unless you speak the language and are prepared to live away from everyday conveniences such as a selection of shops you should expect to pay a premium for having the facilities you need and want. You may see properties advertised for just £15,000 but you will have to pay for restoration and they are unlikely to be in an ideal location.

Most of the tourism in Crete is on the north coast. Although it is mild on the coast in winter it can be snowy inland and in the spring chilly.

While the property market has been opened up to non-Greeks in Crete, in other areas there are restrictions on where foreigners can buy. These are the border areas and you may be required to get permission before buying along the border with Albania, Yugoslavia and Bulgaria and near to the Turkish frontier.

Generally it is not worth buying the cheaper properties (under £10,000) because property like this is likely to be remote and in poor condition making the renovation costs high. As a result you are unlikely to get your money back when you come to sell.

Buying a home

This should be relatively simple (bar any language difficulties) and safe (provided you do not sign anything before getting legal advice).

As in other European countries you will need to use a notary, have a search conducted at the Land Registry, and put down a deposit of between 5 and 30 per cent on the exchange of the preliminary contract.

Buying costs are high with land registry taxes adding 9–11 per cent to the purchase price. Legal fees are usually around £1000. You should budget for around 15 per cent of the asking price to cover taxes and legal fees. It is quite common in southern Europe to try and undervalue the property to save on taxes. But there has been a clampdown on this in many areas with an 'objective value assessment' applied and in other areas revaluations take place at the discretion of the local tax agent. Now that you know you have to pay capital gains tax you should remember that by undervaluing the property when you buy your capital gain will be larger when you come to sell.

There is a form of capital gains tax which is based on inflation — anything you make above the rate of inflation is taxed. But, for instance, if you bought a £100,000 apartment and sold it a year later for £120,000 you would probably get away with £600 in tax. The tax is between 10 and 25 per cent of the difference between the value after the allowance for inflation. It varies depending on how long the property has been owned and the area in which it is situated.

In addition there is an annual property tax which ranges from 1 to 2 per cent and is only applied to individuals owning property of a relatively high value. As a British buyer you will probably not pay this tax unless you own a substantial investment in Greece.

The 'Pothen Esches' referred to earlier is the requirement for Greek buyers to explain where they obtained the funds from to buy a property. It should not affect you provided you import the foreign exchange legally into Greece through the proper banking channels.

Before you part with any money or sign any agreement it is essential that the terms of the transaction are fully understood by you and the vendor. Always put everything in writing as vendors have been known to change their idea of what was 'understood'.

Do not part with a deposit (which you are unlikely to be able to recover) before drawing up a 'pre-contract agreement'. This should not be legally binding but will define the intentions of buyer and seller. Once this has been agreed — and if you have not done so already — you should appoint a lawyer who has a thorough knowledge of Greek property transactions and preferably can speak English or offer an English translation service. In any transaction there should be a lawyer for both parties in addition to the official notary who will handle the transfer of title.

Once the contract is signed and you have paid the deposit (usually 10 per cent but can be as much as 30 per cent), a date for completion will be inserted into the contract. You must be sure that you have the loans agreed or funds available to meet this date as unless the vendor agrees to an extension you will lose your deposit. If you cannot be there in person for the completion you should give your lawyer power of attorney. If you attend you will need an official interpreter so that you are fully aware of the proceedings and understand what you sign.

You will need to provide the balance of the payment plus the notary's fees and official taxes. Monies transferred into Greece had to be certified by the receiving bank until July 1994. This was the only way to take your money out of Greece with ease once you sold. Although this rule has now been relaxed, still check with your bank to avoid any confusion.

At completion the notary will ensure that the vendor has received full payment and simultaneously transfer the title of the property into your name. At this moment it becomes yours — together with any liabilities. That is why it is important to employ a lawyer, for any debts that have not been cleared will now become your responsibility and if a distant relative of the vendor has not had his right to use the property for two weeks each August cancelled you could have an unwelcome guest.

Restoring a home

The market is still in its infancy to the foreign investor and few old properties that have been restored have yet to come back on to the house market.

If you are planning to restore your own home — marble and ceramics are among the many local materials — you should expect to pay an additional 50 per cent on top of the buying price.

Planning permission is fairly straightforward, partly because land in Greece is in plentiful supply. Employ a local architect and builder and make sure the work is overseen.

Building your home

You may see lots of advertisements for building land, which look relatively cheap. The advantage of building a home to your own specifications is that you will get exactly what you want and not suffer the problems of modernising an old ruin.

Costs vary from £50 to £100 per square foot depending on the materials used, and building land from as little as £14,000.

Moving to Greece

You can take all your personal possessions free of taxes if you are planning to move to Greece but must first apply via the Greek Consulate. Correct documentation is important — or else you could end up paying taxes before customs will allow your goods to enter Greece. You will need an itemised list of all goods.

Taxation

If you become resident in Greece you will be liable to tax on your earnings worldwide even if the funds are not in Greece. Non-residents and temporary residents in Greece are taxed only on their Greek earnings. These earnings include rental income. Married persons are taxed separately. Certain expenses including household repairs and furniture are allowable against tax. But under double-taxation agreements you should not have to pay tax on rental income in both the UK and Greece.

Working in Greece

EU nationals can freely enter Greece to look for work and no permit is required. You can stay for up to three months unless you have become a burden on public funds.

Permits

If you stay for more than three months you must apply for a Residence Permit either at the Aliens Department in Athens or at the local police station. You must present your passport, a letter of intent of employment or proof that you can support yourself, and a medical certificate to say that you are not suffering from any infectious diseases. Medical certificates are obtained from a local hospital. Your initial permit will be for six months and after that expires a five-year permit will be issued.

Taking your children

There are foreign schools at both primary and secondary level in Athens and a few other large cities.

Health

Although Greece has over 550 hospitals you may not find that you have adequate medical facilities nearby, particularly if you choose to buy a property on a smaller island. Private health insurance is recommended. And before buying check out local facilities and how quickly you can reach a major hospital in an emergency.

Buying a home in the USA — Florida

I have concentrated on Florida in this chapter because that is where there has been most interest from British buyers wanting a home in the United States.

Florida boasts good facilities, warm weather, a good standard of living and, more importantly, cheap property prices with homes often available with a communal — or even their own — swimming pool and access to a nearby golf course.

Known as the Sunshine State, Florida, on the south-eastern peninsula of the USA, has two coasts: the Atlantic and the Gulf of Mexico. There are nearly 1500 miles of beaches. And the eight-hour flight to Miami, although long, is often not expensive. Florida is on the same latitude as the Sahara giving an average temperature of 80° Fahrenheit and even in winter temperatures are around 64°. And nowhere is further than 80 miles from the sea. More than 20 million tourists visit Disney World each year. Florida attracts over 47 million tourists a year and one in three of these is British.

The main tourist areas are Orlando — with the Disney complexes, the EPCOT Centre, Disney–MGM and the 1.5 million acre Everglades as well as Cape Canaveral. The beaches around Miami on the Atlantic coast are world famous but parts of Miami are out of bounds as it can be a very violent city.

The Gulf coast tends to be quieter and less developed than the Atlantic coast between Miami Beach, Fort Lauderdale and West Palm Beach. Two-bedroom condominiums start at £80,000 upwards. Other Orlando resorts worth looking at are St Petersburg and Clearwater. Tampa is one of the largest ports in the USA and the coast to the north has become more developed.

Florida Keys, the little islands which extend like a string of pearls from the southern tip of Florida, are becoming increasingly popular.

They are connected by 42 bridges and at the end Key West, where both Ernest Hemingway and Tennessee Williams lived, is worth visiting for the entertainers and musicians on Mallory Pier. And the Bahamas, nearby, are also worth a visit.

Warning: Crime in Florida can be a problem. Although there have been several high-profile cases of carjacking and some tourist murders, the situation is not as bad as it seems provided sensible precautions are taken. Follow this Foreign Office advice:

- tourists are easy to spot in hire cars so do not collect one at night;
- do not get out of your car if it is rammed from behind — drive on to a busy area;
- keep to main roads;
- watch out for suspicious people and do not open your door to strangers;
- do not resist a thief;
- carry the minimum amount of valuables with you; and
- do not stop after you have driven away from your car collection point at Miami airport to consult your map — people who do this are known to be targeted by robbers.

How much will it cost?

Thousands of Brits are expected to buy a home in Florida this year, even though the number has fallen dramatically from its peak in the late 1980s when more than 8000 were buying each year. For their first purchase many Brits still head for central Florida around Orlando in the hope of rental income but the Gulf Coast is increasingly attractive.

Unlike many places that attract the British looking for a second home or property investment, Florida has not suffered the same decline in property prices and the high number of US and Canadian nationals relocating to the state has kept the market buoyant. In addition, the rental market is very strong — meaning you can earn money from your home in the months you are not there.

Prices for a substantial home with 1330 square feet of living space and a quarter-acre plot near the Buenaventura Lakes, start at around £60,000 and facilities include golf, swimming pools and tennis courts.

A more luxurious home in Palm Beach ten minutes from the ocean with four bedrooms and three bathrooms set in one and a third acres with pool and jacuzzi will cost around £225,000.

In Clearwater, near Tampa, a large ground-floor apartment in a waterfront complex with pool, tennis and fitness centre will cost around £90,000.

However, it is still possible to pick up a reasonable family home for less than £60,000 for a three-bedroom villa with pool. Apartments in desirable locations can be bought from £45,000.

Buying a home in Florida

There is plenty of consumer protection for those buying a property in Florida. Estate agents — known as real estate brokers — must be licensed. The Florida Real Estate Commission has a code of practice and there are state laws governing professionals involved in the property market. Lawyers (attorneys-at-law) are regulated by the Florida Bar Association. Lawyers are allowed to do the conveyancing and may also be title agents for the purpose of issuing land title insurance; however, they may have to employ a separate title agent to do this. Notaries may be required to witness signatures on some completion documents.

There are currently no monetary exchange controls or restrictions, but there are foreign reporting requirements. US Customs Form 4790 must be completed by those bringing in more than $10,000 in cash. Disclosure forms are usually handled by the professional doing the transaction although the buyer has final responsibility for filing requirements.

Always visit the property first, check building work is of a sufficiently high standard and do not sign anything before consulting a lawyer. A British couple visiting Florida recently decided to buy a property in a development under construction. Unfortunately they did not have the contract they were offered reviewed by a lawyer so they did not spot a clause which allowed the developer to pay their deposit into his general operating funds. When he went bankrupt they lost their $30,000.

Once contracts are signed they are binding on both parties. *Never* pay money directly to a vendor. Instead pay your deposit into a secure *escrow* account which is held by a third party. You will find that brokers are very helpful but, if you want, you can employ a buyer's broker to look after your interest.

Always check what is included in the price from furniture to fixtures and fittings. If you are buying a new property get the broker to check on the progress of building work and inspect the property when it is finished. Brokers should also be able to help you with your mortgage, insurance, tax, visas and even the connection of electricity and water supplies.

The property contract will set out details and conditions and you should get a lawyer experienced in dealing with Florida property transactions to check this. In addition to listing price, terms for payment, restrictions and the exchange date, the contract will also state how costs are divided. You can negotiate these costs as there are no fixed rules. As the contract offers consumer protection it is essential that everything you need to be included is inserted (such as the right to have your deposit returned if your mortgage application is refused).

Check that you have clear title to the property and if you are planning to let out your home (there may be restrictions on how much time you can spend in the USA) check that there are no restrictions on short-term letting. Also make sure that the contract imposes restrictions on the vendor by stating what land and buildings are included and that the property is structurally sound and free from termite infestation.

If you are buying a new property your representative should make a thorough examination and list everything that the builder needs to make good. Make sure that all the building costs have been paid.

You will need to undertake a title search. This is done either by a title company or attorney to check that the seller is the legal owner and that there are no title defects or restrictions or easements (as these could affect your use and enjoyment of the property).

An insurance policy to protect against any future claim on the title from another party is often required by lenders to protect the loan but you should also take out your own.

Several parties get involved in the completion of the transaction which is known as closing or settlement. It is coordinated by the title company, lender, mortgage broker, real estate broker and lawyer. Your lawyer or broker can be appointed to represent you at the meeting. Once clear title has been established and the closing costs are paid plus issuing of the habitation certificate (for a new home), you can assume ownership of the property. In Florida a standard warranty deed is the general means of conveyance of title but does not replace the title examination.

If you do not attend in person you will be sent the documents to study and sign. But first consult your lawyer. The settlement statement lists the services you will receive, costs and money to be exchanged. You should check this before completion. These are points to be aware of, and useful terms:

Fee simple

In Florida a freehold title is usually called fee simple.

Joint ownership

If a husband and wife purchase the property together, they own it as joint tenants and upon death of one, it automatically goes to the other without need for probate. There can be tax consequences, however.

Homes under construction

It is quite common to buy a property that is still under construction or has been completed recently. Special care should be taken to be sure that all the costs of construction have been paid by the sellers. Failure to check this could result in you paying twice for the house due to subcontractors or suppliers having placed a 'lien' on the home as they have not been paid for their services or supplies.

Different types of property

Condominiums

We are not familiar with the concept but in the USA and much of Europe 'condos' are a popular way to buy. Both apartments and houses can be bought on this basis. Unlike the British system you buy your property outright, not on a lease with a fixed term. But you co-own the public areas of the rest of the development and in the case of an apartment, the building and communal areas.

Condominiums are managed by an association of owners with an elected board. Each owner will contribute to the annual maintenance of the complex. The advantage of buying a condo is that you will have someone else to manage the maintenance of the property in your absence. Security will be better than with a detached house on its own. And you will also be able to have facilities that you may not be able to afford if you bought a freehold: most condo complexes have swimming pools and tennis courts.

However, although letting your unit should be no problem, there could be restrictions on the use of the property.

Making money out of your home

Restrictions on letting out property, especially on a short-term basis in some parts of Florida, may mean that you will not be able to finance your property purchase through rental income. Some local authorities limit rentals to less than one or three months and you must have a licence and a licence number as well as charging guests a sales tax on every short-term rental. This applies even if the rental is paid overseas and if you fail to charge it and pay the tax on a monthly basis you could face harsh penalties. However, there is nothing to stop you loaning your home to friends and relatives on an informal basis.

Rental property taxes are charged in addition to income tax. First, there is a personal property tax which is assessed on the value of the tangible personal property. Second, real property taxes are based on the assessed value of the land. There is also a sales tax of 6 per cent on the total rental charge for rental of property of six months or less. Certain states impose additional taxes on short-term rentals.

Raising the money

You should open a US bank account and deposit enough money to meet the costs. To open a bank account you will need your passport and driving licence plus $200. A branch close to your home is suggested. The deposit for your property can then be paid into an *escrow* account (not to the vendor).

Loans are usually restricted to 70 per cent of the property value (and up to 30 years subject to status, *not* age) and your real estate broker will help you to find this finance. The high deposit of 30 per cent is in addition to closing costs, legal and mortgage fees, the fee for your credit report, mortgage insurance, termite inspection, survey of boundaries, valuation, title examination and insurance, closing fee, fees for recording the deed and mortgage, local, county and state taxes and the first mortgage repayment.

Mortgage repayments on property loans including any mortgages you already have in the UK should not exceed 28 per cent of your gross monthly income. In addition you will probably be required to take out mortgage insurance against payment default, life and disability insurance and hazard insurance (like our buildings insurance) against fire and storms. Mortgage arrangement fees include those for your credit report and property valuation (not a full survey).

Running costs

In addition to mortgage repayments if you have them, there are property taxes, insurance, management fees and maintenance costs. The lender will require hazard insurance but you should also take out extra cover for buildings, contents and third-party liability. Make sure that the cover includes times when the property is unoccupied.

All land and buildings in Florida are generally taxed on an annual basis in arrears. This *ad valorem* tax is based on the value of the property and you should find out what this is and if it has been paid for that year (bills are usually sent out on 1 November and have to be settled by the following March) before closing.

Tax

If you spend 183 days or more in any calendar year in Florida, or more than 122 days a year on a regular basis, you are deemed to be resident for tax purposes and pay US tax on your worldwide income. Even if you only spend a few months a year in Florida you will still have to pay tax on any income arising in the USA including rental income as a non-resident alien. The tax year is the calendar year and you can deduct expenses against your rental income to reduce your tax liability, including some of your mortgage interest, maintenance bills and insurance as well as an allowance for depreciation. Under the double tax treaty between the UK and USA you can credit tax paid in the US against your British tax liability.

Remember the Inland Revenue will tax you on your worldwide income including that from overseas properties. Even if this income is not brought back into the UK you will still be taxed in the UK by virtue of your being domiciled here. Report the income and expenses on your tax return and if you have already paid tax on the same income to the USA tax authorities you may claim a Foreign Tax Credit. Mortgage interest on overseas properties is tax deductible and if you make a loss in one year you can carry this forward to offset against the next year of rental profit.

Non-resident aliens are not permitted to file a joint tax declaration and must file separate income tax returns even if the property is jointly owned.

What if I want to sell?

You will be taxed on the profit made when you sell your home as a non-resident alien. You and/or your broker must withhold 10 per cent of the price and pay it to the US revenue; however if the gain is less than this you can apply for a smaller sum to be withheld. The tax on property is covered by the Foreign Investment in Real Property Tax Act of 1980 and is designed to ensure that foreigners do not hold and dispose of US real estate without incurring any US tax.

If you want to apply for a withholding certificate or a reduced tax liability contact the Director, Philadelphia Service Center, PO Box 21086, Philadelphia, PA 19114.

Inheritance tax

Inheritance tax is liable on property owned by a non-resident alien in the USA. An estate tax return (Form 706) is required if the gross value of the property in the US exceeds $60,000. Non-residents are also subject to US gift taxes with an annual exclusion of $10,000 per donee. Above this level rates range from 18 to 55 per cent.

Visa and residence

If you only wish to spend up to 90 days in the USA you do not need a visa. If you wish to stay up to six months you will require a B1/B2 visa. However, it is much harder to obtain permanent residence — the 'green card' — as you will need to be sponsored by a close family member who is a US citizen or permanent resident and this could take a long time. An individual may qualify as a resident of Florida without having obtained US citizenship. An appropriate visa is required and international residents can file a declaration of domicile.

If you succeed in this you have many benefits including a tax exemption allowance to offset against taxes, free education through to the 12th grade and generally speaking no personal state income tax, and no estate and probate tax.

Visas should be obtained through a reputable Visa consultant.

Other countries of interest to British homebuyers

The main countries of interest to British homebuyers looking for an overseas property have been covered in their own chapters.

Only a limited number of buyers purchase homes in the following countries and as such these sections go into less detail. In many cases foreign ownership of property is restricted.

- Andorra
- Austria
- Cyprus
- Germany
- Gibraltar
- Malta
- Switzerland

Andorra

A landlocked co-principality in the Pyrenees surrounded by France and Spain, Andorra is most popular as a ski resort. It is also a tax haven with no income tax, no capital gains tax and no inheritance tax, but there are plans to tighten up its use as a tax haven. Andorra is no longer the tax haven it once was. The appeal of owning a property in the principality is that you pay no taxes if you are a resident. In the past you could become a resident if you had sufficient funds on deposit in Andorra. Now you are assessed before becoming a resident. You can opt to be a member of an Andorran company to avoid paying taxes. However, if you work outside Andorra you will pay tax. If you retire in Andorra and are not earning income elsewhere you will not have to pay taxes. It does not have its own currency but uses the French franc and Spanish peseta.

Around 1000 Brits live in Andorra and less than 10,000 of the population of 50,000 is Andorran so the overseas market is well established. To be granted a residence permit applicants must own or rent a property in Andorra and have private medical insurance — only those under 65 are eligible to join the social security system. Catalan, French and Spanish are the main languages.

Credit Andorra (tel: 00 336628 20326) can provide mortgage loans and multi-currency accounts.

A property can be reserved verbally but as in other European countries, once your deposit of 10 per cent has been placed with the vendor's agent you must go ahead with the purchase or lose your deposit.

You will need a lawyer as well as a notary who will handle the conveyance. Notaries charge around 1 per cent of the purchase price. You will also need a 'suplica' which is an official formality giving the government permission to buy or sell a property. It takes up to two weeks for it to be granted.

Estate agency fees are often included in the price. New residents also pay a one-off levy varying from £5 to £25 per square metre.

Prices start at around £40,000 for a very small one-bedroom ski apartment or studio.

The main residential districts include Arsinal, Erts, La Massana, Sispony, Sant Julia (which is much warmer than the others) and Ordino. Every property in these areas is within 15–30 minutes of the main town centre which is Andorra La Vella, the main shopping area where property is very expensive.

A three- to four-bedroom chalet or house costs around £275,000. A town or terraced house known as an 'adosado' with four bedrooms will cost between £150,000 and £175,000. Apartments with two bedrooms and two bathrooms start at £80,000.

There is a restriction on foreign ownership with only one property allowed per person or couple of up to 1000m square. The only taxes are the local community rates which vary from commune to commune and tend to be between £70 and £150 a year. There is also a tax charged on the head of the family which is around £75–£100 a year.

Austria

This is another country that will appeal to those who love skiing and other winter sports. However, few Britons have bought here even though the Austrian Alps are very popular with tourists from the UK. Part of the problem is the shortage of properties and escalating house prices. Also, it is virtually impossible to purchase property in some regions if you are not Austrian.

In the centre of Austria the Styrian Salzkammergut district is open to the British with one-bedroom apartments on sale for around £35,000–£40,000.

A lawyer will act for both sides, deposits are not normally necessary and documents are signed before an official of the Austrian Embassy. Costs are around 8 per cent of the price.

Cyprus

This has long been popular with the British, many of whom lost money when the island was partitioned in 1974 following the invasion by Turkish troops. It declared independence from Britain in 1960 but has continued to have strong links with us and English is spoken by practically everybody (partly thanks to the local British forces and English language TV programmes).

The south of the island is the Greek Cypriot Republic of Cyprus and the north the self-proclaimed Turkish Republic of Northern Cyprus. Cyprus is the third largest island in the Mediterranean with a population of around 700,000.

Half of all tourists (some 800,000) are British. Most visit the southern Greek Cyprus which has a booming tourist trade with miles of high-rise hotels in many resorts. However, it is still possible to buy a quiet villa away from the noise of tourists but near enough to local facilities.

Although the northern part of the island is now attracting more tourists if you are looking to buy a property, the Greek side of the island will probably be the safest option.

There are two airports — Paphos and Larnaca — and the main business centre is Nicosia, the capital. Larnaca, Limassol and Paphos on the south coast are the main resorts.

Aside from its long links with the British, Cyprus has many other attractions for the British property buyer — 320 days' sunshine a year, English is widely spoken, there are good beaches, the Mediterranen sea, as well as temperatures reaching 90° Fahrenheit in August and inland there is a mountain range where it is possible to ski in winter.

Flights take three and a half hours to Larnaca and and four hours to Paphos.

Where to buy

There are restrictions on foreign ownership which limits purchase to one villa or apartment building and to a land area not exceeding 28,800 square feet. Your choice will depend on what sort of lifestyle you are looking for.

Nicosia: the capital city and a very busy and bustling one at that. But you will probably not want to buy here.

Limassol: the main port which is also quite busy and has good shopping facilities. But again, the large number of hotels that stretch for miles along the coastline may mean it will not be what you are looking for.

Larnaca: also has a large number of hotels and apartments, an airport and is the fourth largest town.

Paphos: is slightly smaller. Twenty years ago it was a small fishing village but now it is a major resort. Ayia Napa is another small fishing village that has also become a major tourist spot.

Remember, buying a property in a tourist area will mean that the area is very crowded in peak season and deserted in low season and there has been substantial development which can make some resorts look a bit like those on the Costa del Sol. So a home in a village is often the best option and these types of properties are the ones that appeal most to British buyers.

Prices

These vary depending on how much work needs to be done to the property and its location and distance from the beach.

Prices start from around £30,000. A two- to three-bedroom villa can cost anything between £100,000 and £150,000. If it is on the coast it can cost anything between £75,000 and £160,000. In a residential area away from the coast you can buy a similar property for between £45,000 and £100,000. Of course prices will be lower if you buy an unmodernised home.

It is quite common to buy from a developer who will tailor the property to your specificiations.

How to buy

The legal system is based on the English and Welsh. You should employ a lawyer. Property is registered at the local Land Registry. You will sign a preliminary contract which is binding on both sides and is subject to your getting good title on the property and obtaining the required permits. The lawyer or notary lodges the deposit, searches are carried out by your legal adviser and then an application must be made to the Council of Ministers — a requirement for all non-Cypriots who want to purchase property — and you will have to prove that you have sufficient income or assets and no criminal record.

Permission normally takes 8–14 months to be granted and without this title deeds cannot be made available to the purchaser. Individuals cannot get permission for more than one property and generally permission will not be granted if the property is to be used for letting to others on a commercial basis. Once searches have been carried out, the final contract is signed and lodged with the Land Registry (which should be done within two months of being signed). This will prevent the vendor from selling the property a second time.

A permit is then required from the Central Bank to allow the transfer of the purchase money (this application is not required if both the vendor and purchaser are foreigners).

Costs should not be more than 10 per cent of the purchase price and include stamp duty (roughly 0.15 to 0.2 per cent), Land Registry fees (5 to 8 per cent), lawyer's fees (1 per cent), application to the Council of Ministers (£200 sterling) and local authority taxes for street lighting and refuse collection (£30–£100 Cypriot pounds a year depending on the size of your property). An annual immovable property tax is also levied, based on the value of the property (rates are between 2 and 3.5 per cent per £1000 of value with cheaper properties exempt). Most of these costs bar the Land Registry fees are very small.

You are required to pay for your property in a foreign currency. Personal cheques, bankers' drafts and telex transfers are all acceptable.

Tax

Tax is charged on income you bring into Cyprus. It means that those retiring to Cyprus face a tax of around 3 per cent on their income and around 5 per cent on investment income. Capital gains tax is charged at around 20 per cent. However, there is a double taxation agreement with the UK to ensure that you are not taxed twice and CGT is not charged if the property was acquired by the importation of foreign currency. The low income tax regime can be very beneficial, particularly if you are retiring to Cyprus. As long as you do not return to the UK for more than 90 days a year, you will be taxed at the Cypriot rate of 3 to 5 per cent. You can also buy a new car duty free — almost halving the costs charged in the UK (and there is an extra bonus — in Cyprus they drive on the left!) Estate duty/inheritance tax is rarely paid as it is not charged on property outside Cyprus and on assets within the country there are generous allowances. From April 1997 the estate duty law is being abolished and after that date there will be no estate duty payable whatsoever.

Residence permits

These can be obtained on proof that you own a property in Cyprus and are self-supporting.

Renting out your home

Foreigners are not allowed to let their property to holidaymakers; however, many do.

Other useful information

The UK and Cyprus have a social security agreement covering National Insurance including pensions and other benefits. Contact the DSS (see Useful Addresses) for relevant pamphlets and information.

Germany

Few British go to live in Germany unless they are posted there with their jobs, the forces or by the Diplomatic Corps. However, the single European market means that more and more firms are now operating across borders. Germany has a comparatively low level of homeownership compared to the rest of Europe — around 40 per cent — and most of those moving to Germany would probably consider renting rather than buying. However, if you are considering buying these are the basic things you should know.

Germany has a big emphasis on order, rules and regulations and German law requires that everything is written down.

If you intend to stay more than three months you will need a residence permit — 'Aufenthaltserlaubnis'.

Estate agents should be able to lead you through the buying process; however, you will need a lawyer.

Property is recorded in a Grundbuch at the Grundbuchamt — similar to our Land Registry. This will tell you who owns the property; its description and details of debts — property must be sold free of liabilities.

As in most other European countries a notary (notar) vets, signs and witnesses the contract. The fee is 5 per cent plus VAT.

Gibraltar

As Gibraltar is a British crown colony not only its language but its laws and culture are still very British, even though it is surrounded by Spain and the subject of much diplomatic debate between the two countries.

Its population of 28,000 is crammed into a tiny space of just two square miles. Population density is 4319 per square kilometre making it one of the most crowded spots in Europe.

It is a tax haven and 70 per cent of its employment remains in the public sector. There is no VAT but there is estate duty on property of between 5 and 25 per cent as well as property rates and duty on imported items of 12 per cent (but personal effects are excluded).

Some 6000 expats live on 'the rock' as it is known (it is dominated by a 430 metre high block of limestone) and EU citizens are entitled to live and work there. Property is scarce and can be expensive, with apartments from £60,000 for the very smallest. Please note, the UK does not treat Gibraltar as though it is another EC country for healthcare. Visitors can get urgent treatment but residents should join the Gibraltar scheme or get private cover.

How to buy a property

Buying a property is similar to procedures in England and Wales (Gibraltar law is based on English Common Law). Employ a solicitor for the conveyancing. Stamp duty is 1.26 per cent of the price of the property. There are also small land registry and land title registration fees.

Property in Gibraltar is registered on a property register in much the same way as in the United Kingdom.

Unlike in other European countries, you can (as in England and Wales) withdraw from the property purchase at any time until the contracts are exchanged without losing your deposit (usually 10 per cent). The words 'subject to contract' should be included in your offer. As in the UK, check what fixtures and fittings are included in the purchase price at the time you make the offer. The seller's lawyers will provide your lawyer with proof that the vendor owns the property and your lawyer will make enquiries regarding the property (as in the UK) including questions on ownership of boundaries, alterations to the property etc. Local authority searches should also be conducted to check on any relevant planning consents. And you should also arrange for a structural survey. Arrange your finance before exchange of contracts as these are binding.

There are several major building societies and banks in Gibraltar who will lend mortgage finance, usually up to 85 per cent of the valuation of the property.

Costs

Stamp duty is payable on the purchase of property at the rate of £12.60 for every £1000 of the price paid and at £1.30 for every £1000 secured by the way of mortgage deed. You will also have to pay Land Registry and supreme court fees (currently £40 each).

Tax

Gibraltar is a tax haven and there are no double taxation agreements between it and any other country. This means that your financial affairs in Gibraltar are kept secret — the authorities are not required to disclose them to any other tax authority.

There is no capital gains tax payable in Gibraltar when you dispose of an asset at a gain. High net worth individuals will also find the tax system advantageous as there is a limit on the maximum amount of income tax paid (currently £17,500) for those who qualify under this legislation.

Malta

This island too, has long been popular with the British. English is widely spoken and there have been historical links between the two countries. Some 4000 Brits own property here. The Maltese archipelago is strategically placed between Europe and North Africa and gained independence from the UK in 1964. Tourism is Malta's chief source of income with an influx of tourists each year of over two times the island's population. Gozo, the smaller of the two main islands, has a slightly different climate to Malta and is far greener. Malta itself tends to be more barren, particularly nearer to the coast. Valletta is the capital city with a large harbour and along the coast there are many bays (although not many beaches) and smaller marinas full of expensive yachts.

The climate is similar to that of Greece with at least six hours of sunshine a day — even in winter.

Some 450,000 tourists from the UK visit every year. Water is desalinated and as a result you will be paying out for bottled water if you do not like the taste. Most goods including oil and much food is imported.

Buying a property

Non-Maltese are restricted to buying properties worth more than £30,000 (approximately £15,000 Maltese). You do not pay any tax on a holiday home.

Foreigners must apply to the Ministry of Finance for an AIP permit which allows you to purchase a property. You will be restricted to buying only one property on Malta or Gozo, the purchase money must originate outside Malta and the property must not be bought for renting out. The house purchase procedure is similar to that of the UK with a few exceptions — mainly that the preliminary agreement is binding on both the vendor and purchaser. A notary public is employed to draw up a preliminary agreement and this is signed by both parties. You must then pay your 10 per cent deposit. Searches are then carried out to check for defects in the title or any liabilities. However, searches do not cover future development plans — these must be checked at the Public Works Department. Your funds must then be transferred and the Central Bank of Malta will have to be provided with evidence that these have come from outside Malta.

The costs to budget for include: stamp duty, 1 per cent notarial fees, 10 per cent deposit and search, registration and Ministry of Finance fees of £100 Maltese. Lawyers' fees will be around 1 per cent of the purchase price. Estate agent's fees are usually paid by the vendor. You will also have to pay local rates.

Prices

An apartment reasonably near the coast will cost around £36,000 sterling (unfurnished).

A detached house in a relatively smart area will cost around £200,000 sterling and a semi-detached home £160,000 sterling. A converted older property will cost around £70,000 sterling. Further away from more popular areas prices drop to around £50,000. On Gozo, which is reached by ferry, prices tend to be slightly cheaper.

The best places to buy include Bugibba, Xemxija, Qawra and Mallieha, according to the Association of Malta Estate Agents. Sliema and the surburb of St Julians and the inland towns of Rabat, Medina and Mosta are all popular.

Permits and residence

If you plan to stay in Malta for more than three months you will need to apply to the immigration authorities to renew your visa or you can apply for residency. You need to write to the Expatriate and Nationality Division of the Office of the Prime Minister in Valletta. If you want to become a permanent resident (and take advantage of Malta's low rate of income tax) you will need to prove that you have an income of around £20,000 sterling a year or that you have capital of £240,000 sterling, although this does not have to be in Malta. You have to bring in a further £12,000 sterling plus £2000 for each dependant. If you qualify you will be granted special taxation terms with a flat rate tax of 15 per cent on income brought into Malta (once allowances have been taken into account).

Taxes

If you live in Malta for more than six months in any one calendar year you will need to apply to become a temporary resident and will then have to pay income tax on income brought into the country (less personal allowances). Taxes start at 10 per cent and there is an annual allowance similar to that in the UK. Death duties have been abolished and capital gains tax is calculated only on gains made since January 1993.

Moving

You can import household and personal effects free of duty and a car can be imported within six months of arrival.

Renting out your home

As a non-Maltese you can only do this if you have a privately owned swimming pool (not a shared one) and you apply for a licence. Applications must be made through a Maltese managing agent.

Switzerland

It is difficult for non-Swiss to buy properties in Switzerland and there are restrictions in each canton (county) as to the number of foreign homeowners allowed. This varies from region to region and there is usually a waiting list.

In any given year as few as 130 British buy a property in Switzerland. Despite these restrictions some 15 per cent of the total population is made up of non-Swiss. Fewer than 2000 foreigners are allowed to buy in Switzerland each year.

Even if you manage to buy, you are restricted to one property per family and you are locked into the property for ten years minimum (but certain cantons will allow you to sell after two and five years provided you sell to a Swiss national). You are unlikely to make a profit on your property, but exchange fluctuations could work in your favour.

The Swiss had been planning to bring in a law allowing foreigners to sell to other foreigners without authorisation or restriction. However, this has now been shelved and restrictions on foreign ownership still vary on a canton by canton basis. Some cantons have relaxed the ten year rule on ownership. In Canton Vaud and Canton Fribourg, foreigners no longer need to keep property for a set number of years and in Canton Valais, the number of foreigners allowed to buy property has been increased, however homes must still be owned for a minimum of ten years. It is easier to buy in the French speaking cantons although a few German speaking cantons are now allowing foreigners to buy properties and in some mountain areas foreign ownership is allowed but only of properties above a certain price level.

Switzerland was effectively closed to foreign home buyers until 1979 and then properties had to be owned for ten years. So only in the last few years have there been the first resales of properties. There is a large price gap between new homes and resale homes (which are much cheaper). This combined with exchange rate fluctuations means that properties are now relatively cheap.

Some properties are now half the price they were three years ago. A studio can be bought from just £23,000 in Leysan, one bedroom apartments start at between £35,000–£40,000 and even chalets can be bought from £100,000.

It is not difficult to get hold of Swiss properties and there are many on the market, according to agents Villas Abroad who report that most sellers are open to offers. But buyers must be prepared for the fact that in some cantons they must keep the property for ten years and they may have high annual outgoings. Switzerland is not a tax haven. VAT of 6.5 per cent is charged on building materials, but not on the land, but this will only affect new homes adding 2–5 per cent to the purchase price. Legal fees, land tax and registration fees will add a further 2.5 per cent.

New properties are more expensive — for instance an older chalet which would cost around £150,000 will be about half the price of a new one.

The cost of living is very high as are the living standards. Taxes of 0.5 per cent per annum of the value of the property are payable to the commune, canton and Swiss government.

Residence rights are not granted automatically to those who own property in the country.

If you do succeed in being able to buy a home, you will need a barrister (rechtsanwalt or avocat: remember German, French and Italian as well as Rhaeto-Romanic are spoken in Switzerland) as well as the services of a notary, who will handle the conveyancing.

Useful addresses

Addresses for general advice and finance

Abbey National *(for overseas mortgages)*
Abbey House
Baker Street
London
NW1 6XL
Freephone 0800 449090

Blackstone Franks
Investment Management Ltd *(for advice on tax planning and useful guides to living abroad)*
Barbican House
26-34 Old Street
London
EC1 9HL
0171-250 3300

British Association of Removers & Federation of International Furniture Removers
3 Churchill Court
58 Station Road
North Harrow
Middlesex
HA2 7SA
0181-861 3331

BUPA International
Russell Mews
Brighton
BN1 2NR
01273 323563

Department of Health Leaflets Unit
PO Box 21
Stanmore
Middlesex
HA7 1AY
0171-210 4850

Department of Health Information Service
Freephone 0800 66 55 44

Department of Social Security
Overseas Branch
Benton Park Road
Newcastle upon Tyne
NE98 1YX
0191-213 5000

Department of Social Security
Pensions and Overseas Benefits (Payments)
Tyneview Park
Whitley Road
Benton
Newcastle upon Tyne
England
NE98 1BA
0191-218 7777

Department of Social Security
Leaflets Unit
Hannibal House
London
SE1 6LZ
0171-210 3000

FOPDAC
Federation of Overseas Property Developers, Agents & Consultants
PO Box 3534
London
NW5 1DQ
0181-941 5588

Inland Revenue *(for booklets)*
Public Enquiry Room
Inland Revenue
West Wing
Somerset House
London
WC2R 1LB
0171-438 6420

Inland Revenue *(for payments of pensions & dividends overseas)*
Inspector of Foreign Dividends
Inland Revenue
Fitzroy House
PO Box 46
Nottingham
NG2 1BD
0115-974 2000

Institute of Chartered Accountants
Chartered Accountant's Hall
Moorgate Place
Moorgate
London
EC2P 2BJ
0171-920 8100

Insurance:
Andrew Copland
(International Insurance Specialist)
230 Portland Road
London
SE25 4SL
0181-656 8435

Law Society
113 Chancery Lane
London
WC2A 1PL
0171-242 1222

Ministry of Agriculture, Fisheries and Food
(for guidance on taking your pets overseas)
Government Buildings
Toby Jug Site
Hook Rise South
Tolworth, Surbiton
Surrey
KT6 7NF

Private Patients Plan International
Crescent Road
Tunbridge Wells
Kent
TN1 2PL
01892 512345

Property Owners Club
Brittany Ferries
Millbay
Plymouth
PL1 3EN
0990 143555 (premium higher charges)

Royal Institution of Chartered Surveyors
12 Great George Street
London
SW1P 3AD
0171-222 7000

Timeshare Council
23 Buckingham Gate
London
SW1E 6LB
0171-821 8845

Useful reading material

World of Property Magazine
(Also publishers of *Focus on France*)
532 Kingston Road
Raynes Park
London
SW20 8DT
0181-542 9088

International Property Magazine
Top Floor
2a Station Road
Gidea Park, Romford
Essex
RM2 6DA
01708 450784

Living France (magazine)
Subscriptions
USM Distributions Ltd
86 Newman Street
London
W1P 3LD
0171-396 8068

Removal firms specialising in International moves

Note: This list gives only a selection — always check that the firm you use has insurance and is a member of the Overseas Group of the British Association of Removers.

Arts International
Ditchling Common Industrial Estate
Hassocks
West Sussex
BN6 8SL
01444 247551

Burke Bros
Fox's Lane
Wolverhampton
WV1 1PA
01902 729030

Richman-Ring Ltd
International Movers
Eurolink Way
Sittingbourne
Kent
ME10 3HH
01795 427151

Simpsons of Sussex
Units 1, 2 and 3
Tidy Industrial Estate
Ditchling Common
Hassocks
West Sussex
BN6 8SL
01444 871800

The Old House
London office
0181-947 1817
South coast office
01323 892934

White & Company Plc
Hillson Road
Botley
Southampton
SO30 2DY
01489 788096

Useful addresses for each country

France

French Embassy
58 Knightsbridge
London
SW1X 7JT
0171-201 1000

French Consulate-General
21 Cromwell Road
London
SW7 2EN
0171-838 2000

The French Tourist Office
179 Piccadilly
London
W1V 0AL
0891-244 123 *(premium higher charges apply)*

In France:

Her Britannic Majesty's Embassy
35 Rue du Faubourg St Honore
755008 Paris
00 331 42 66 91 42

Consular Section (General)
9 Avenue Hoche
75008 Paris
00 331 42 66 38 10

Franco-British Centre
8 Rue Cimarosa
75116 Paris
45 05 13 08

British Institute
11 Rue de Constantine
75008 Paris
45 55 71 99

Banque Woolwich *(part of the Woolwich Building Society)*
2nd Floor
34 Boulevard Malesherbes,
75008 Paris
00 331 47 42 55 61

The Mediterranean Property Owners Association
00 331 93 87 57 09

French property agents

Note: This is a selection and not intended as a comprehensive list — generally you will find a good selection of French 'agents immobiliers' in the area of France you are interested in.

La Residence *(for northern and south-western France)*
27 High Street
Benson
Oxon
OX10 6RP
01491 838485

French Property News
2a Lambton Road
Raynes Park
London
SW20 0LR
0181-944 5500

Properties in France *(for the West and Loire Valley)*
34 Imperial Square
Cheltenham
Glos
GL50 1QZ
01242 253848

Cottages in Rural France
Church Road
Swanmore
Southampton
Hants
SO3 2PA
01489 893677

A House in France
11 Mountview
Mill Hill
London
NW7 3HT
0181-959 5182

Villas Abroad
(also for Switzerland and Andorra)
100a High Street
Hampton
Middlesex
TW12 2ST
0181-941 4499

Legal advisers

John Venn & Sons
95 Aldwych
London
WC2B 4JF
0171-395 4300

Russell-Cooke, Potter & Chapman
2 Putney Hill
London
SW15 6AB
0181-789 9111

Spain

Spanish Consulate-General
22 Manchester Square
London
W1M 5AP
0171-589 8989

Spanish Embassy
39 Chesham Place
London
SW1X 8SB
0171-235 5555

British Embassy in Spain
Fernando el Santo 16
28010 Madrid
00 34 1 31 90 200

British Consulate General
Madrid
Centro Colon
Marques de la Ensenada 16
2 Piso
28004 Madrid
00 34 1 308 5201

(British Consulates are also found in Barcelona, Bilbao, Ibiza, Las Palmas, Malaga, Mallorca, Santander, Seville, Tarragona, Tenerife and Vigo)

Blackstone Franks — Spain
Avenida de Mijas, No 18
Edificio Alegria III
1st Floor
Apartado de Correos 108
29640 Fuengirola
Malaga
00 34 52 479710
(Also has offices in Alicante, Mallorca, Tenerife)

Legal advisers who specialise in Spanish law

Note: This is not a comprehensive list and you are recommended to contact the Law Society.

John Howell & Company
17 Maiden Lane
Covent Garden
London
WC2E 7NA
0171-420 0400

Michael Soul & Associates
21 Gough Square
London
EC4A 3DE
0171-353 3358

Diaz-Bastien & Truan
111 Park Street
London
W1Y 3FB
0171-491 3308

Fernando Scornik Gerstein
3rd Floor
32 St James's Street
London
SW1A 1HD
0171-930 3593

Spanish property agents

David Scott International
Deerhurst House
Epping Road
Roydon
Harlow
Essex
CM19 5DA
01279 792162

Steve Williams
International Property Consultants
(IPC)
45 Devon Road
Cheam
Surrey
SM2 7PE
0181 642 4376
(Costa Blanca, Tenerife and The Canaries)

Ian Lawrence
Prime Property International
7 High Street
Maidenhead
Berkshire
SL6 1JN
(Costa del Sol)

Adrian Medd
European Villas
195 Chesterton Road
Cambridge
CB4 1AH
01223 514241
(Costa Blanca and Minorca)

Italy

Italian Embassy
14 Three Kings Yard
London
W1Y 2EH
0171-312 2200

Consulate-General
38 Eaton Place
London
SW1X 8AN
0171-235 9371

Her Britannic Majesty's Embassy
Via XX Settembre 80a
00187 Roma
00 39 6 475 5441/5551

British Consulate-General
Via XX Settembre 80a
00187 Roma
00 39 6 475 5441/5446

Italian lawyers

Dr Claudio del Giudice
Bishopsgate House
5–7 Folgate Street
London
E1 6BX
0171-377 1138

Property agent

Brian A French & Associates Ltd
22–26 Albert Embankment
London
SE1 7TJ
0171-735 8244

Useful reading material

Belle Cose Magazine
12 High Street
Knaresborough
North Yorkshire
HG5 0EQ
01423 865892

Portugal

British Embassy in Lisbon
Rua S Domingos a Lapa 35-37
Lisbon

British Community Council
Rua S Sebastiao Pedreira 122-3
Lisbon

British Association Oporto
Rua Infante D Henriques 8
Oporto

Portuguese Consulate-General
62 Brompton Road
London
SW3 1BJ
0171-581 8722

Portuguese Chamber of Commerce
1–5 New Bond Street
London
W1Y 9PE

Portuguese Embassy (Chancery)
11 Belgrave Square
London
SW1X 8PP
0171-235 5331

Portuguese National Tourist Office
22–25a Sackville Street
London
W1X 2LY
0171-494 1441

Algarve Resident Magazine
39 Rua 16 de Janiero
No 6, 8400 Lagos
00 351 82 342936/341813

TAP Air Portugal
Fares and ticketing
38–44 Gillingham Street
London
SW1V 1JW
0171-630 0900

Property agents in England include:

European Villas
195 Chesterton Road
Cambridge
CB4 1AH
01223 514241

Legal advisers specialising in Portugal include:

Cornish & Co
Lex House
1–7 Hainault Street
Ilford
Essex
IG1 4EL
0181-478 3300

Greece

Greek Embassy/Greek Consulate General
1a Holland Park
London
W11 3TP
0171-229 3850

Greek National Tourist Organisation
4 Conduit Street
London
W1R 0DJ
0171-734 5997

174 / Buying Abroad: A Country-by-Country Guide

Property agents

Clare Developments International Ltd
Pen Lea
Arkell Avenue
Canterton
Oxon
OX18 3BS
01993 842597

Brian A French & Associates Ltd
See page 171.

Florida

American Embassy
Grosvenor Square
London
W1A 2JB
0171-499 3443

Property agents & mortgage advice

Sunstate International
272 Wallisdown Road
Bournemouth
Dorset
BH10 2HZ
01202 546622

Bill Hartman
Hartman Homes Group
10 The Plateau
Warkfield Park
Berks
RG42 3RH
01344 886832

Tax consultants specialising in Florida

Lee Churchett
(UK and US tax, specialising in those buying and letting property)
The White House
13 Lansdowne Road
South Woodford
London
E18 2AZ
0181-530 3966

Andorra

Andorran Delegation
63 Westover Road
London
SW18 2RF
0181-874 4806

Credit Andorra
Avinguda Princep Benlloch 19
Andorra la Vella
Andorra
00 33 37 6 203226

Property agents

Le Griffon
PB 78 Poste Française
Andorra la Vella
Andorra
00 33 6 8837169

Villas Abroad
100a High Street
Hampton
Middlesex
TW12 2ST
0181-941 4499

Austria

The Austrian Embassy and Consular Section
18 Belgrave Mews
London
SW1X 8HU
0171-235 3731

Cyprus

Cyprus High Commission
93 Park Street
London
W1Y 4ET
0171-499 8272

Legal advisers

Cornish & Co.
See page 173.

John Howell & Co
See page 169.

Germany

Embassy of the Federal Republic of Germany
23 Belgrave Square
London
SW1X 8PZ
0171-235 5033

Visa and passport department
0171-235 0165

Coton, Kilgore & Lavigne *(lawyers)*
Hamilton House
1 Temple Avenue
London
EC4Y 0HA
0171-353 1101

Gibraltar

Gibraltar Tourist Office
4 Arundel Great Court
179 Strand
London
SW1X 7JT
0171-836 0777

Abbey National Gibraltar Ltd *(building society)*
237 Main Street
Gibraltar
00 350 76090

Cornish & Co *(lawyers)*
1–7 Hainault Street
Ilford
Essex
IG1 4EL
0181-478 3300

Malta

Malta High Commission
16 Kensington Square
London
W8 5HH
0171-938 1712

Association of Malta Estate Agents
7 Whispers
Ross Street
Paceville
Malta
00 356 337 373

Expatriate and Nationality Division
Office of the Prime Minister
Valletta
Malta

Cornish & Co (Lawyers)
See above.

Switzerland

The Swiss Embassy
16–18 Montagu Place
London
W1H 2BQ
0171-723 0701

Villas Abroad
See page 167.

Osbornes Solicitors
93 Parkway
London
NW1 7PP
0171-485 8811

Index

accountants 22
   fees 16
addresses, useful 160–77
administrative hassles 14–15
agents, renting out through 23
   France 103–4
agreements, formal, and holiday lets 25
air travel, to France 79
Algarve 124–6
Alps, French 83–4
Andorra 148–9, 175
apartments, Spain 56
Austria 149–50, 175

Balearic Islands 52–3, 76
bank accounts
   France 100
   Portugal 130
   Spain 64–5
bed and breakfast, as alternative to holiday lets 24
bedlinen, and holiday lets 24
benefits *see* social security benefits
bereavement, and retiring abroad 28
births, registration
   France 103
   Spain 73

British Association of Removers, address 33, 72
British holidaymakers, renting out to 23, 103
Brittany 84–6
building own home, Greece 138
buildings, illegal, Spain 62–3
Burgundy region 89
buying v. renting 14, 19

Calabria 113
Campania 113
Canary Islands 54–5, 63
capital *see* finance raising
capital gains tax 23
   Cyprus 152
   France 97–8
   Gibraltar 155
   Greece 136–7
   Italy 115, 116–17
   Portugal 131
   Spain 66–7
caretakers 22–3
cars
   France 102, 105–6
   Italy 122
   and moving abroad 32, 35
   Portugal 131–2
   Spain 75
Charente Maritime region 88–9
children 15

Spain 71
see also education
cleaning, and holiday lets 24
climate, and retiring abroad 27, 80
communal ownership
   Portugal 127
   Spain 56
condominiums 20, 25
   Florida 144–5
   France 90, 102
consumer rights, Spain 57–9, 74
coproprietes, France 90, 102
Costa Almeria 51–2
Costa Blanca 48–50
Costa Brava 50
Costa Calida 51–2
Costa de la Luz 51
Costa del Sol 47–8
Costa Dorada 50
costs 16–17
   see also purchase costs; running costs; taxes
crime, Florida 141
cultural considerations 14, 15
   France 77
customs duty on belongings 31–2
Cyprus 150–3, 176

death duties
   Portugal 131
   see also inheritance tax
death of partner 28
deaths, registration
   France 103
   Spain 73
dentist, need to inform 35

Department of Social Security (DSS) 34–5
   address 27, 35, 72
developers, and financing purchase 18
doctor, need to inform 35
domicile status 38
Dordogne region 88–9
double taxation treaties 38
   Cyprus 152
   France 96
driving 32, 35
   in France 79–80, 82, 102, 105–6
   in Portugal 131–2
   in Spain 74–5
DSS *see* Department of Social Security

education 15, 29–30
   France 107
   Greece 139
   Spain 73
Elba 114
electrical items 31
electricity
   France 107
   Italy 118, 119
   Portugal 130
   Spain 76
EU citizens' rights 27, 30
   working within EU countries 71, 92, 132, 139
European Council of International Schools, address 73
exchange control, Spain 70
exchange rates 17
existing UK home, selling 17

Index / 181

family considerations 15
 see also children; education
family law *see* inheritance law
fee simple, Florida 144
finance raising 17–18
 Florida 145–6
 France 101
 Italy 120
 Spain 65, 66
financial contacts, informing 34
Florida 140–7
 useful addresses 174–5
Foreign Investment Tax Act, US 147
France 33, 77–108
 area profiles and prices 81–90
 buying process 92–5
 pros and cons 77–8, 79–80
 renting out 103–5
 running costs 95–103
 useful addresses 165–8
 where to live 78–9
freehold property 21
 Florida 144
friends, renting out to 23
Fuerteventura 55
furniture, and moving abroad 31, 33

gas services
 France 107
 Italy 118
 Portugal 130
 Spain 76
Germany 153–4, 176
Gibraltar 37, 154–5, 176–7
gifts tax, France 99
Gran Canaria 55
Greece 33, 134–9

 area profiles and prices 135–6
 useful addresses 173–4

health 14, 27, 36
 France 106
 Greece 139
 Italy 121
 Portugal 132
 Spain 72, 73
holiday homes, basics 22–5
holiday lets 23–5
 Cyprus 153
 Florida 145
 France 103–4
 Malta 158
 Spain 68, 70
holidaymakers, letting to British 23, 103
homes overseas *see* ownership types
housekeepers 22

Ibiza 53
ICI (Italian tax) 117
identity cards
 Italy 121
 Portugal 132
illegal buildings, Spain 62–3
illness *see* health
import duty 31–2
 Portugal 130
income, and retiring abroad 26–7
income tax 37–8
 Cyprus 152, 153
 France 96–7
 Gibraltar 155
 Italy 117–18
 Portugal 131
inflation 17

inheritance law
  France 102–3
  Italy 120–1
  Spain 73–4
inheritance tax 39
  Cyprus 153
  Florida 147
  France 96, 98–9
  Spain 69
Inland Revenue, need to inform 34
insurance 16, 27
  Florida 146
  France 101–2
  Italy 122
INVIM (Italian tax) 116–17
IRPEF (Italian tax) 117–18
Italy 33, 109–22
  area profiles and prices 109–14
  legal procedures 114–16
  running costs 116–18
  useful addresses 171–2
IVA (Italian VAT) 115, 116
IVA (Spanish VAT) 63, 69

joint ownership
  Florida 144
  France 91
journey times, France 79–80

La Gomera 55
La Palma 55
land registry tax
  Cyprus 152
  Gibraltar 155
  Greece 136–7
land tax, France 99
languages, importance 14
  France 77
  Portugal 133
  Spain 72
Lanzarote 55
Latium 112
Law of Horizontal Ownership, Spain 56
Le Marche 111–12
legal procedures
  Cyprus 151–2
  Florida 142–4
  France 92–4, 102–3
  Gibraltar 154–5
  Greece 136–8
  Italy 114–15
  Malta 156
  Portugal 126–9
  Spain 57–63
letting out *see* holiday lets
Ley de Costas, Spain 62
Liguria 112–13
loans 18
  see also mortgages
local taxes
  France 99
  Italy 118
  Portugal 129–30
  Spain 68–9
local representatives 17, 22
  Spain 70
Loire Valley 89
Lombardy 112
loneliness, and retiring abroad 28
long-term renting 14, 19

maintenance 14–15, 16
  condominiums 20, 144–5
  Spain 56, 64

Index / 183

Majorca 52–3
Malta 155–8
  useful addresses 177
medical considerations *see* health
Minorca 53
mortgages 18
  Florida 146
  France 101
  Spain 65, 66
moving house
  practical problems 31–3
  to Greece 138–9
  to Italy 121
  to Malta 157
  to Portugal 130
  to Spain 72
  useful addresses 160, 164–5
municipal taxes *see* local taxes

nationality
  French, acquisition 103
  Spanish, acquisition 71
new homes, building
  Florida 144
  Greece 138
Normandy region 86–7
north coast of France 84–7
Northern Spain 52

officials, Spanish 74
offshore companies 37, 69
optician, need to inform 35
ownership types 19–21
  condominiums 20, 90, 144–5
  freehold 21, 144
  joint ownership 91, 144
  renting 14, 19
  timesharing 20–1, 57, 90–1

Paris 89–90
partner, death of 28
Pas de Calais region 87
pensions 26–8
  France 106–7
  Italy 122
  Spain 72
permits
  Cyprus 153
  Florida 147
  France 91–2
  Germany 154
  Greece 139
  Italy 120
  Malta 157
  Portugal 131, 132
  Spain 70–1
pets, and moving abroad 32–3, 132
Philadelphia Service Center, address 147
'plus valia' tax, Spain 67–8
Portugal 33, 123–33
  areas and prices 124–6
  useful addresses 172–3
post office, need to inform 35
prices 15, 16
  Balearic Islands 53
  Canary Islands 54, 55
  Cyprus 151
  Florida 141–2
  France 77
    northern 85, 86, 87
    southern 81, 82, 83, 84
    western 87, 88, 89
  Greece 135
  Italy 109, 110, 111, 112, 113, 114
  Malta 157

184 / Buying a Property Abroad

Portugal 125–6
Spain 44, 48, 49, 50
Switzerland 159
professional advisers, informing 34
property purchase overseas, pros and cons 13–15
property purchase process *see* finance raising; legal procedures; purchase costs
property tax
   Cyprus 152
   Florida 145
   Greece 137
   Spain 68
property types
   Florida 144–5
   Spain 56–7
pros and cons of buying abroad 13–15
pueblo-style property, Spain 56
purchase costs 13–14, 16–17
   Cyprus 152
   France 94–5
   Gibraltar 155
   Greece 136
   Italy 115–16
   Portugal 129–30
   Spain 63–4, 66
purchase process *see* finance raising; legal procedures; purchase costs
purchase finance *see* finance raising

rail travel, France 80
refuse collection
   Italy 118, 119
   Portugal 130

registration tax, Italy 115
removers 16, 31, 33
   Spain 72
   useful addresses 160, 164–5
renovation
   Greece 138
   Italy 119–20
   Portugal 130
rental property tax, Florida 145
renting v. buying 14, 19
renting out *see* holiday lets
residence permits *see* permits
restoration *see* renovation
retiring abroad 26–8
   to Spain 71–2
rooms, renting out 24
running costs
   Florida 144, 146
   France 90, 95–102
   Greece 137
   Italy 116–19
   Portugal 129–30
   Spain 64, 66–70
   see also taxes
rural France 88–9

sales tax, Florida 145
Sardinia 113
savings 17
second homes, basics 22–5
second mortgages 18
security, and retiring abroad 28
selling property 23
   existing (UK) home 17
   Florida 147
   France 98, 105
   Greece 137
   Portugal 130–1
   Spain 63, 65, 67

service charges
  France 90
  Italy 116
services *see* utilities
sickness *see* health
Sicily 113–14
SISA (transfer tax), Portugal 129
social life, and retiring abroad 28
social security benefits 36–7
  Cyprus 153
  France 106–7
  Italy 121
  and retiring abroad 26–7
  Spain 72, 73
south of France 81–3
Spain 33, 43–76
  area profiles and prices 47–52
  legal procedures 57–63
  property seeking 44–7, 56–7
  purchase costs 63–4
  running costs 64–70
  useful addresses 168–70
  see also Balearic Islands; Canary Islands
stamp duty
  Cyprus 152
  France 94
  Gibraltar 155
storage of belongings 31
succession tax *see* inheritance tax
surveys, structural
  France 95
  Portugal 127
  Spain 62
Switzerland 158–9
  useful addresses 177

tax avoidance
  Andorra 148
  France 100
  offshore companies 37
  Spain 69
taxes 16, 22, 23, 32, 37–8, 39
  Andorra 148
  Cyprus 152–3
  Florida 146–7
  France 94, 95–100
  Gibraltar 154, 155
  Greece 136–7, 139
  informing Inland Revenue 34
  Italy 115, 116–18
  Malta 157
  on pensions 27
  Portugal 129–30, 131
  Spain 63, 64, 66–70
telephone services
  and holiday lets 24, 104
  France 108
  Italy 119
  Portugal 130
  Spain 75
Tenerife 54–5
timeshare 20–1
  France 90–1
  Spain 57
Timeshare Council, address 20
transfer tax, Portugal 129
travel cost considerations 17
travel firms, renting out through 24, 104
travel times, France 79–80
trusts 37
Tuscany 109–11
TV licences, Italy 118
TVA (VAT in France) 94, 98, 105

Umbria 111
United States *see* Florida
urban France 89–90
utilities
   France 95, 107–8
   informing UK suppliers 34
   Italy 118–19
   Portugal 130
   Spain 64, 75–6

VAT (value added tax) 32
   France (TVA) 94, 98, 105
   Italy (IVA) 115, 116
   Portugal 129
   Spain (IVA) 63, 69
Vehicle Licensing Centre,
   informing 35

Veneto 112
villa-style property, Spain 56
visas *see* permits

water services
   France 107
   Italy 110
   Spain 76
wealth tax, Spain 68
west coast of France 87–8
wills 38–9
   France 102
   Portugal 133
   Spain 74
working
   in Greece 139
   in Portugal 132
   in Spain 71

Index of Advertisers

Abbey National (Gibraltar) Ltd 8
Andrew Copeland Ltd 7
Frank Salt Real Estate Ltd 6–7
John Howell & Co 63
Spanish Legal Services 45